How God Answers Your Prayers

Randy Petersen

with Christine A. Dallman

Publications International, Ltd.

Randy Petersen is a writer and church educator from New Jersey with more than 40 books to his credit, including *Why Me, God?* and *God's Answers to Tough Questions.* A prolific creator of church curriculum, he's also a contributor to the *Quest Study Bible,* the *Revell Bible Dictionary,* and the iLumina Bible software.

Christine A. Dallman is a freelance writer living near Everett, Washington. She is the author of *Daily Devotions for Seniors,* an inspirational resource for maturing adults, as well as co-author of several other PIL titles.

Louis Weber, CEO
Publications International, Ltd.
7373 North Cicero Avenue
Lincolnwood, Illinois 60712

Permission is never granted for commercial purposes.

ISBN-13: 978-1-60553-928-7
ISBN-10: 1-60553-928-7

Manufactured in U.S.A.

8 7 6 5 4 3 2 1

Contents

God Delights in Helping Us

"God help me!"

You've probably heard that phrase uttered in times of need. The idea is usually this: *We've done all we can to manage our messy situation, and if things get any worse, then God help us! We can only hope that God will work some kind of miracle.*

God help us! God help *me!* Each of us seriously needs the God of heaven to reach down to earth and rescue us from our problems and even ourselves. We've tried every solution we can think of, and still we need help. Will the almighty Creator look down in mercy and offer a little assistance?

Yes! That's what God does. He loves to help people who need it. The overwhelming message of the Bible is that he *longs* for human beings to reach out to him. When we ask for his aid, he is delighted to help us.

The problem is that we don't ask for his help enough. "You do not have, because you do not ask," the Bible tells us (James 4:2). We feel too shy, or too distracted, or too determined to fix things on our own, and so we

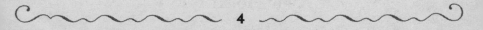

never make the request. "God help me!" When you think about it, that cry is the supreme act of faith. We are saying that we need help and that we trust God to provide it.

This book is about what happens next.

When we ask for God's help, how does he respond? In what ways does he offer aid? And, as we observe these patterns, how will that affect our prayers? We could ask God to help us win the lottery, and he probably won't—not because he doesn't love us, but because he does.

What can we learn about God's mysterious ways? And how can this understanding draw us closer to him?

While this book starts with problems, it moves quickly to a more positive tone. God is active in and around us, and he will surprise and delight us in many ways—if we're paying attention. These pages are full of biblical insight—promises and challenges alike—and accounts of real people who asked God for help and got it. For privacy, some names have been changed, and details have been altered, but the stories are true. God has worked in amazing ways— and he will continue to do so in your life, too.

Chapter 1
VERY PRESENT

One Sunday late in 2007, a troubled young man went on a shooting spree in Colorado Springs, Colorado. He first went to a missionary training center and then a church parking lot, killing two at each site and wounding several others. At the church, a security guard named Jeanne Assam saw the shooter walking down a hallway toward her, armed with multiple weapons.

People were running in panic, but Assam drew her pistol and hid, waiting for the right moment. She also asked God for help. "I was given the assignment to end this before it got too much worse," she said. "I just prayed for the Holy Spirit to guide me. I said, 'Holy Spirit, be with me.'"

When the gunman came close, she confronted him, identified herself, and shot, wounding him. The man then fatally shot himself. Jeanne Assam was hailed as a hero. Her courageous action saved the lives of many at the church.

"I give the credit to God," she said. "My hands weren't even shaking."

Most of us will never have to rely on God's help in such a dramatic way, but we do rely on him. Whether we're battling illness, a bad habit, or an economic downturn, we ask God for help. Most of us will never need to confront killers, but we could be studying for a test, driving through a snowstorm, or trying to put a baby to bed. When we ask the Lord for help, he regularly provides healing, strength, and support.

"God is our refuge and strength," the psalmist declares, "a very present help in trouble" (Psalm 46:1). That's what you want from God—his presence. If you ask your teenage son to help you paint the house, you need him to be there and not off somewhere on his cell phone. It's no wonder, then, that the adjective used for the assistance offered by the omnipresent God is *present*. He's here for us, seeing our need and stepping in to help.

Scholars tell us that the Hebrew word used here for *present* can also mean *proven*. God has come through time and time again, not only for you and me but also for many generations of believers. God has a lengthy track record, an impressive résumé.

Let's say you give up on painting your house and decide to hire a professional. You call a company and ask, "What work have you done before? How long have you been in business?"

If they reply, "Well, we just started painting houses last month, because it seemed like fun. We've never really had any clients before." Chances are, they won't get your business.

But at the next company you call, they say, "We're fourth-generation house painters, learning the craft from our great-grandparents. We've had thousands of satisfied clients." Their track record inspires trust.

The same thing is true with God. For millennia, people have sought his help and received it. "Therefore we will not fear," the psalmist continues, "though the earth should change, though the mountains shake in the heart of the sea; though its waters roar and foam, though the mountains tremble with its tumult" (Psalm 46:2–3). The world as we know it could be falling apart, but we rest in the confidence that God almighty is our refuge and strength. He will surely provide the help we need.

Except when his answer is "no."

Not Whether but How

For every testimonial of a prayer miraculously answered, there's another story of a request denied. We may say blithely that God answers all our prayers, but we must admit that sometimes his answer is "no." God helps us in our need, but he doesn't always give us the help we seek. It would be dishonest to say otherwise. The Bible itself has multiple examples of people who *didn't* get what they asked from God.

Often you'll hear an athlete thanking God after a big game. "I just want to give all the glory to God for enabling me to do what I did out there today." There's nothing wrong with this, except that it begs a question: *Wasn't God enabling the other team, too?* Surely there were athletes on the losing side who prayed for strength. Did God deny their petitions?

Most devout athletes have figured this out. They know God doesn't really care who wins the game, but they ask for God's help in doing their best. The Lord gives strength to players on both sides and lets them fight it out themselves.

Would this same principle apply, then, when nations go to war? Or when two companies bid on a lucrative contract? Or when several candidates apply for the same job? Or when students compete for a scholarship? We instinctively pray for victory, for us getting what we need to move ahead with the kind of life we want. But if God says "yes" to us, he might have to say "no" to someone else who wants the same thing.

The point is that God's help is more complex than we might imagine at first. It's not a question of *whether* God helps us—he can and he does—but *how* he does so. Many of us have come to expect God to fix things for us, to reward us for holy living, or at least to calm us down when things go wrong. When he chooses to help us in a different way, we get upset. *Where is God when we need him? Why isn't he helping?* Suddenly the "very present help in trouble" seems absent. But he's not. He's there and he cares and he helps us, but we need to recognize the complex ways he provides that help. When we dig into these complexities, we may learn to pray in a whole new way.

Happy are those whose help is the God of Jacob,
    whose hope is in the Lord their God,
who made heaven and earth,
    the sea, and all that is in them;

who keeps faith forever;
> who executes justice for the oppressed;
> who gives food to the hungry.

The Lord sets prisoners free,
> the Lord opens the eyes of the blind,
> the Lord lifts up those who are bowed down,
> the Lord loves the righteous.

The Lord watches over the strangers
> he upholds the orphan and the widow,
> but the way of the wicked he brings to ruin.

—PSALM 146:5–9

Dear Father, thank you for your wisdom
that sees and takes into consideration
what I ask you for but that, in perfect love,
always gives me what is best for me and
what will benefit my life most in the long
run. Help me remember that your answers
are never confined to my expectations
or to the possibilities I can see. Your
limitless resources can bring guidance and
provision from places I'm not even aware
of right now. Help me remember, too, that

your will is for me to be transformed into Christ's image, and not that everything goes my way. Today help me lay down any impatient expectations and demands I may be making of you—consciously or unconsciously—and release the outcomes of my circumstances to you.

Mr. Fix-It

We live in a push-button culture. Do you want to cook some food? Just push a few buttons on the microwave and—*voila!*—a hot meal is provided. Want to talk to a friend across the country? Just push a few buttons on your cell phone. One mother was amused recently when her children rode with their aunt in her 15-year-old car. The kids were fascinated by the roll-down windows, since they had known only push-button automatic windows. "Cool!" they said. "Could we get these rollers on our car?"

Computerization has only intensified our dependence on immediate solutions. In fact, "push-button" will soon become an outdated concept, as computers learn to recognize our voices, remember our preferences, and seemingly read our minds. You'll be able to tell your TV-computer the name of any movie ever made, and it will appear.

So it only makes sense that God would be like that. If he is a "very present help in trouble," then wouldn't he immediately respond to our needs, like some heavenly vending machine dispensing the assistance we need? That's what we assume, and that's how we pray: *Lord, give me strength. Lord, give me the words to say. Lord, find me a parking place.*

Sometimes we have it figured out, how our problems will be solved, and we give God a specific order: *Lord, please make sure I get that raise, so we can move to a bigger house, and there will be more room for the kids, and they won't get on my nerves so much.* Sometimes we have no idea how God will solve our problems—we just expect him to figure it all out: *I have too much stress, Lord. Please make my life easier!*

Is it wrong to pray these prayers? No, of course not. God loves to hear from us. "Do not worry about anything," the Apostle Paul encourages, "but in everything by prayer and supplication with thanksgiving let your requests be made known to God" (Philippians 4:6). Sometimes God gives us exactly what we ask for. He *does* fix things for us—on occasion. But sometimes he chooses to do something else—either to solve our problems in a different way or to solve different problems.

It's a bit like going to the doctor. You might show up and say, "I'm getting migraine headaches. Give me some of those new migraine pills." And maybe your physician will do exactly that, writing out the prescription you want. Or maybe she'll say, "The headaches are intensified by your high blood pressure, which you have because you weigh too much. The best thing you could do is lose 20 pounds. Here's a diet and exercise plan to get you started." Is she a bad doctor if she doesn't give you the pills you want? No! In fact, you might say she's a better doctor because she's looking out for your entire well-being.

And is God any less caring because he doesn't always fix your problems just the way you want?

It would not be better if things happened to men just as they wish.

—HERACLITUS, *FRAGMENTS*

How good you are, heavenly Father, to look at the whole picture of my life in the scope of eternity as I cry out to you from my tiny viewpoint of the here and now! When I whine that things aren't to my liking, Father, you listen, and yet you remind me that complaining doesn't help, but instead that I need to look to your Word to know your will for me. Such a humble attitude puts me in the right place to receive your answers— answers that get to the primary issues of my life instead of the superficial symptoms of my deeper needs. How incisive your Word is! How insightful your Spirit, my counselor! Help me listen today as you speak words of healing and life to me.

Happy are those whose strength is in you, in whose heart are the highways to Zion.... They go from strength to strength.... For the Lord God is a sun and shield; he bestows favor and honor. No good thing does the Lord withhold from those who walk uprightly. O Lord of hosts, happy is everyone who trusts in you.

—PSALM 84:5, 7, 11–12

Magic Words

As we've just seen, there are problems with the view of God as Mr. Fix-It—the push-button, vending machine approach that expects him to instantly do whatever we ask. But there's a common variation on that theme that carries its own dangers. In this view, God is sort of a genie in a bottle. You know the old story: Someone rubs a magic urn and out pops a genie who promises to grant three wishes. Yet there are always complications. Usually there's some magic incantation involved. The person needs to word the wishes just right.

We often get kind of "magical" in our reliance on God's help as well. That is, we expect God to grant our pleas if we pray the right way or live the right way. The implication is that God owes us. We do something for him, and he'll do something for us.

"For six months I've been praying for a friend who has cancer," says Jack, "but there's still no progress. And I'm not just praying, I'm fasting once a week. Every Thursday, no solid foods, just liquids. Yet now I'm wondering if maybe I'm doing it wrong. Maybe I shouldn't even drink liquids when I fast."

First, let's acknowledge that Jack is very committed. Second, there is a long-standing connection between prayer and fasting. It might seem like a strange concept to some, but fasting is a way to demonstrate—to ourselves and to God—that he is more important to us than anything else, even the basic necessities of life. In a way, fasting flushes out our priorities, helping us focus on God's desires more than our own.

So Jack's dedication to prayer and fasting is admirable, but there's still a problem. If Jack is using fasting as a way to get God to do what he wants, he's missing the point. That would be a bribe, an effort to manipulate God. The same might be said for any vow we make in an effort to get our God-genie to grant our wish. "If you do this, Lord, I swear I'll never smoke/drink/lie/lust/swear again."

Good living is its own reward. Such vows may be valuable as a way of connecting with God in a deeper way, but if we expect God to pay us back by answering our prayer, then aren't we being manipulative?

Children try this with their parents all the time. "You're the best parents in the whole world! Can I have a pony? I'll clean my room every day." Of course, wise parents see right through such tactics. Sure, they want the kid to clean up, but not just to get a pony.

When we treat God this way, the focus is on us, whether we're saying the right words or doing the right thing. But God operates by grace. He shows us his kindness according to his will. Yes, he wants us to ask him for things, but he also wants us to care about what *he* wants for us.

If people treat God as a magic genie who you have to ask just the right way, what happens when they don't get what they ask for? They turn it back on themselves—like Jack, who worried that he might be fasting the wrong way. He'd been going without food once a week for six months, and *still* he fretted that it wasn't good enough! *If only I was holier,* someone might say, or *if only I knew how to pray better.* They analyze what went wrong with the transaction. Instead, they should be seeking to know God better: *If God chooses to do something other than what I requested, what can I learn about his desires? How can I draw closer to God's heart?*

My Lord, please shift my focus from my desires to yours. I don't want to treat you like a vending machine or some cosmic butler that I expect to bring me whatever I request. Forgive me if that's the way I've been praying. I want to pay attention to what you want. Sure, I have my ideas about the best way to improve my situation, but I know that you have far better ideas. I'm trusting you to apply your awesome wisdom. So teach me your ways. Tune my heart to harmonize with yours.

Lord, you have been our dwelling place in all generations. Before the mountains were brought forth, or ever you had formed the earth and the world, from everlasting to everlasting you are God. You turn us back to dust, and say, "Turn back, you mortals." For a thousand years in your sight are like yesterday when it is past, or like a watch in the night.... So teach us to count our days that we may gain a wise heart.... Let your work be manifest to your servants, and your glorious power to their children. Let the favor of the Lord our God be upon us, and prosper the work of our hands—O prosper the work of our hands!

—PSALM 90:1–4, 12, 16–17

Beyond Your Wildest Dreams

So far we've been discussing false expectations. People often expect God to act as a Mr. Fix-It or a genie, and they get upset when he doesn't. But how *does* he help us? What *can* we expect? How does this "very present help in trouble" work?

In his epistle to the Ephesians, Paul included two amazing prayers. In one prayer, he included this benediction: "Now to him who by the power at work within us is able to accomplish abundantly far more than all we can ask or imagine, to him be glory in the church and in Christ Jesus to all generations, forever and ever. Amen" (Ephesians 3:20–21).

This gives us a crucial clue. The Lord doesn't just give us what we want. He's not just some kind of Santa Claus, going through our wish lists. He goes beyond all that, *far* beyond all that, *abundantly far* beyond all that. He's dealing with things we can't even imagine!

Maybe God is saying something like this to Jack, as he fasts and prays. "Jack, I know you care deeply about your friend with cancer, and I appreciate the seriousness you've shown in your prayers. You want me to heal her, here and now, but let me tell you what I'm going to do. All the suffering she's experiencing now will be turned around in heaven. She will experience bliss with me forever. Every day for eternity will be full of excitement and joy in my loving embrace. Because of her suffering, she will know me in a deep, deep way, understanding the suffering I've been through, and this will create a sense of connection between us that will last forever. Because you have chosen to suffer with her now, you will join in that eternal bliss as well."

It's always risky to put words in God's mouth, but we're in the realm of imagination here. Scripture promises that God accomplishes things beyond our imaginings, and we're just guessing at what those things might be.

Perhaps God is saying, "You've asked me to heal your friend's body, but I'll do even better. I'll heal her soul. She will draw so close to me in her dying days that others will see a radiance within her. They will be drawn to me because of the utter peacefulness of her spirit. I will heal her body eventually, when she joins me in heaven, but right now I have a bigger healing to do. I will bring wholeness to her heart."

When we ask God to fill an order according to our specifications—treating him as a fixer or genie—he may very well respond, "Is that all? There's so much more I want to do for you!" When God doesn't help us in exactly the way we want, it's usually because he's doing something even better for us.

Dear Lord, when I get fixated on my to-do list for you, I lose sight of the fact that you have a beyond-my-wildest-dreams blueprint you're working from for my life—a plan that spans time and eternity, not just a plan to part the traffic jam I might be sitting in at a given moment. I know it's not that you're unconcerned about what troubles me in my day-to-day circumstances, but you also want to lift my eyes to what lies beyond where I'm standing, even beyond my life here. As I consider these things, heavenly Father, I feel like letting go of my list and releasing it to flutter away in the wind. Your plan is all encompassing; my list is too small. Come lead me into the fullness of your awe-inspiring plan.

I have been driven many times to my knees
by the overwhelming conviction that
I had nowhere else to go.

—ABRAHAM LINCOLN

Power Play

Let's take another look at that prayer that Paul prayed. God accomplishes these things "by the power at work within us." It's no surprise that God is powerful. We look at the world he has created and marvel. We wait out a thunderstorm and witness the awesome display of light and sound. Even if we understand the physics of it all, it's still stunning to us, especially when we recognize how commonplace these displays are. To God, it's nothing special. He's just doing his thing.

The surprise we find in Paul's prayer is that this power is also "at work within us." Somehow the creative force of the Almighty One is inside us. And this is not an isolated reference. Elsewhere Paul says,

"If the Spirit of him who raised Jesus from the dead dwells in you, he who raised Christ from the dead will give life to your mortal bodies" (Romans 8:11). Resurrection power is *in our bodies*. This fits with what Jesus promised his disciples when he told them of the Spirit's coming. "Very truly, I tell you, the one who believes in me will also do the works that I do and, in fact, will do greater works than these" (John 14:12).

So this is one way the Lord helps us: *He empowers us*. We may be asking for him to work his magic— snap, snap—to transform our situation, but he may reply, "You do it. I'll give you the power to act with strength, confidence, decisiveness, whatever is necessary. You will transform this situation."

We've all heard of those dramatic cases where, say, a mother lifts a car off of her child. In extreme situations, adrenaline kicks in, and we can do amazing things without thinking about it. But God's empowering doesn't have to be similarly dramatic.

One man (we'll call him Ray) had been praying for a friend of his for several years (we'll call the friend Julie). In a previous conversation, Julie remarked that she didn't think she could ever feel loved by God, because of all the stuff she had done. So as he went through his daily prayer list, Ray began asking God to "show Julie your unconditional love." Then one day Ray learned about something nasty that Julie had said about him. He was hurt, and he wasn't sure how to handle the situation, but later that day, going through his prayer list, he prayed, "Lord, show Julie your unconditional love." He had said this a hundred times before, but this time it was as if God was saying audibly to him, "You do it. *You* show her my unconditional love." In that moment, he was empowered, not only to forgive Julie, but also to do something kind for her.

Sometimes we are the answers to our own prayers. Not because God is playing hooky, but because he prefers to work that way. He delights in doing his work through us.

Thus, if you're asking for God's help to get that raise in order for you to move to a new house so the kids will have room to play and won't get on your nerves as much, don't wait for God to brainwash your boss. Instead, trust in God's power to help you work harder to impress your boss (or to budget more wisely or to raise your kids with more understanding or to cope better with stress). God empowers us in many ways, and that power can transform our situations.

God also *illuminates.* "The Lord is my light and my salvation," the psalmist sings (Psalm 27:1). This is a common theme throughout Scripture. "I will lead the blind by a road they do not know," the Lord said through Isaiah. " . . . I will turn the darkness before them into light" (Isaiah 42:16). He is in the business of enlightening us.

Often the help we need from God is clarity. We don't know what to do, and we desperately need guidance. Or we think we know exactly what needs to be done, but then the Lord illuminates the situation, and we see an entirely different course. In many of these cases, the Lord brings people into our lives to advise us. Sometimes he allows events to transform our thinking. Even if these events are inconvenient or painful, they can "turn on the lights for us" and show us how things really are.

Franny had already gone through a lot of training as an actor, but she was still insecure about her ability. When she had an opportunity to study at a prestigious institute in Paris, she grabbed it. That turned out to be a big disappointment. Though she was ready to learn, the training was beneath her, the sort of thing she had already picked up years earlier. Far from home, having expended money and time, and feeling very lonely, Franny began to wonder if this was all a big mistake. Had she misunderstood God's plans for her?

It was then that the Lord began shedding his light on the situation. She realized that she could be confident in her ability. She had already received all the training she needed, and she could now move on into a professional career, but she might never have seen that without the Paris fiasco.

As he directs our lives, God often leads us along the scenic route. He doesn't usually take us directly from point A to point B. He transports us to places with a good view.

Keep your lives free from the love of money and be content with what you have; for he has said, "I will never leave you or forsake you." So we can say with confidence, "The Lord is my helper; I will not be afraid. What can anyone do to me?"

—HEBREWS 13:5–6

You have called me to walk with you, Lord, and to work with you. You call me to come to you, to take your yoke upon me, and to learn from you. It isn't burdensome, this work to which you call me. In fact, it is an honor and a privilege to participate with you in my development as your child—in learning your ways, in developing the character of Christ in my life, and in becoming all that you mean for me to be. It is a great adventure to walk with you in this way, Lord—challenging at times—but you always give me everything I need to do what you call me to do. It's a journey I wouldn't trade for anything.

The world is sown with good; but unless
I turn my glad thoughts into practical
living and till my own field,
I cannot reap a kernel of the good.
—HELEN KELLER, *OPTIMISM*

Another way God helps us is this: *He opens hearts.* Sometimes he opens our own hearts, and sometimes he opens the hearts of others. Maybe you have already experienced this. Painful experiences can soften us up, making us less self-assured and more open to God. When families or close friends go through trying times, their hearts can open up to one another. There's a sort of pruning process at work there. If relationships are built on fun and good times, they might not survive the hard times. But solid relationships can deepen during hard times.

Rachel was devastated by her divorce. Twenty years of marriage were gone in an instant. She didn't know how she would survive. But, in the desolation that followed, she found herself doing something she hadn't done for years. She prayed.

To be honest, she wasn't really sure there was a God, or if there was a God, she doubted that he would answer her. But her need had cracked open her heart, and she was ready to try anything. She ventured to a church and found some friends who truly cared. They listened to her woes and wept with her. And they joined her in praying for God's emotional healing.

At this writing, she's still in pain, but she's surviving. God is slowly bringing her back to wholeness. There are some glimmers of joy in her life. But more than anything, God has helped her by opening her heart, touching her there, and showing her that he is present.

Lord God, I need your help today. I need you to change my situation, and I realize that might involve changing me. Open my heart. Let your amazing love flow to me and through me. I want other people to know that you are helping me. Restore to me the joy of living, and let my sorrow be an occasion for growth. In this difficult time, I ask you to draw me ever closer to you. Help me know you better. I will give you all the glory as long as I have breath. Amen.

Chapter 2
A Holy Terror

What in the world is going on?

No, really. What *in the world* is going on? Our planet has become a terrifying place. This began to happen even before the infamous events of 9/11, but the years since then have seen a steady escalation of worrisome events.

Whatever illusions Americans had about their own invulnerability were shattered by the 9/11 attacks on the World Trade Center and the Pentagon. The nation hurtled into a War on Terror, and the resulting stress seeped into our everyday lives. We suddenly had to go through extra security checks at airports, and now we eye strangers with suspicion. When mysterious samples of anthrax were mailed to certain prominent figures, we feared that chemical warfare had begun.

As if global terrorism wasn't enough, we've also been treated to a heightened awareness of environmental woes. Scientists talk about global warming and a host of assorted natural disasters. Melting icecaps, they say, will put coastal regions underwater. Changing temperatures will instigate violent storms. Hollywood rushed to illustrate the worst-case scenarios in a torrent of disaster films—so we could vividly imagine the latest theories about the destruction of the world as we know it.

Then the economy tanked. A bubble burst on Wall Street, and irresponsible investment practices were exposed. Respected investment firms went out of business. Banks needed bailouts. Despite the unprecedented influx of government money, pensions and nest eggs were lost. Money that people depended on for their retirement vanished. The housing market froze, and both home and company bankruptcies exploded across the nation. Other companies tightened their belts, laying off workers and dropping needed benefits.

And, as if we needed a fourth horseman of the Apocalypse, we got a plague riding in. The H1N1 virus arrived and was quickly dubbed a pandemic. It didn't take much to stress nerves that had been frayed by terrorism, environmental dangers, and money woes.

If ever we needed God's help, it's now.

He will cover you with his feathers,
　　and under his wings you will find refuge;
　　his faithfulness will be your shield and rampart.
You will not fear the terror of night,
　　nor the arrow that flies by day,
nor the pestilence that stalks in the darkness,
　　nor the plague that destroys at midday.
A thousand may fall at your side,
　　ten thousand at your right hand,
　　but it will not come near you.

—PSALM 91:4–7 (NIV)

Handle with Prayer

So how does God help us in these situations? And how should we pray for his assistance? We could ask God to do a major reversal of all these factors: *Lord, please put an end to terrorism! Please protect the earth you have created! Please restore our economic fortunes! Please eradicate disease!* Can God accomplish these things? Certainly, but it's never a question of ability. The question is: *How does God choose to work in our world?*

The answer to this question is not easy to understand, but our Creator generally opts for stealthier methods. Granted, we are on the way to an eternal kingdom in which all these woes will be erased—"Death will be no more; mourning and crying and pain will be no more" (Revelation 21:4)—but we're not there yet! We live in an in-between time, when God allows the world to suffer the consequences of sin and decay. We are invited to pray, "Thy kingdom come," begging for the rapid arrival of that glorious future, but we are also warned that we'll have to wait for it. The Apostle Peter assured his impatient readers that "the Lord is not slow about his promise, as some think of slowness" (2 Peter 3:9), but that he works on a different schedule. "Do not ignore this one fact, beloved, that with the Lord one day is like a thousand years, and a thousand years is like one day" (verse 8).

So God will answer those mega-prayers (stopping war, disease, etc.) in his future kingdom, but how does he help us in the meantime? Short of overturning the whole problem, what sort of assistance will he offer now? And how should we pray?

We could ask for personal deliverance from these problems: *Lord, protect my loved ones as they travel. Keep them far away from the designs of terrorists. Lord, prevent my employer from laying me off. Lord, keep my family healthy.* There is nothing wrong with these prayers, but we shouldn't be shocked if God doesn't comply. Jesus said that God "sends rain on the righteous and on the unrighteous" (Matthew 5:45). We sometimes fantasize about a world in which good people like us are insulated from the problems everyone else has. While God sometimes provides extraordinary deliverance to his faithful ones, it's more likely that instead he will provide strength to handle the difficulty.

One Tuesday morning Todd Beamer boarded a plane in Newark, headed to San Francisco, but he never made it. The date was September 11, 2001. Todd was on Flight 93, which went down in rural Pennsylvania. An upstanding Christian, a loving family man, active in his church—why wouldn't God protect him from the danger of terrorist attack?

We may never know why, at least until we ask God face to face. Todd's death was certainly a tragedy on a terribly tragic day. He left behind a pregnant wife and two young children. We would certainly hope that God would spare this father with so much to live for, but God did something else. He gave Todd strength in a challenging situation.

Several passengers tried to make phone calls in those last minutes. Somehow Todd got connected with a customer service rep for the airline, and he asked her to call his wife and say he loved her. He talked about a plan that some of the passengers were hatching, a plan to jump the hijackers and retake the plane. It would certainly be dangerous—at least one passenger was already dead—but Todd and others summoned the courage. "Are you guys ready?" the customer service rep overheard Todd say over the open phone line. "Let's roll." The details are still somewhat sketchy, but it appears that he and other passengers fought the hijackers of their plane and prevented them from reaching their target.

At one point Todd's voice was heard saying, "We're going down! Help me, Jesus!" That brings us back to our main question: How did the Lord help Todd Beamer and the many other devout believers who died in the attacks of that fateful day? Did he spare them from harm?

No. Christians don't have a "Get Out of Danger Free" card. Sometimes they die tragically, and their families grieve, but that does not mean God is absent. "We all knew what kind of person Todd was," his wife said later. "We know he's in heaven. He was saved."

Saved is an interesting word to use in this context. No, the flight was not saved—though the Capitol or White House might have been. No, Todd Beamer's life was not saved—at least not his earthly life. But this man had a relationship with a living God that transcended physical death. Through faith, he had eternal life. When Christians use the word *saved,* they generally refer to a spiritual condition—that is, redeemed from eternal damnation—but there's even more to it. Our eternal life has already begun! We are living on this earth with the values and expectations of a God-filled forever. So even when we face heartache, suffering, and physical death, we are "saved" from a meaningless existence. "Just knowing that when the crisis came up he maintained the same character we all knew, it's a testament to what real faith means," said Todd's widow.

God will not always choose to rescue us from tragedy, but he regularly chooses to help in other ways, shoring up souls and relationships, providing strength, comfort, and understanding in the hardest of times.

Heavenly Father, thank you for all the ways you intervene in our lives to give us what you know is best. Sometimes we try to tell you the kind of help we think you ought to provide. But you are the one who made us and the one who knows our truest and deepest needs. We're often like children who believe with all our hearts that what we need is an ice-cream cone, when really what we need is a nutrient-rich meal.

I call you my Father because I trust your all-knowing perspective and believe you will care for me in ways that are ultimately loving. So I pray that when, from my perspective, your path for me seems puzzling, disappointing, or even hurtful, I will choose to continue trusting in you. May I even learn to praise you when, instead of cookies and cream, life is serving up Brussels sprouts and liver. Thank you, Father. You are always good to me.

It is you who light my lamp; the Lord, my God, lights up my darkness. By you I can crush a troop, and by my God I can leap over a wall. This God— his way is perfect; the promise of the Lord proves true; he is a shield for all who take refuge in him. For who is God except the Lord? And who is a rock, besides our God?—the God who girded me with strength, and made my way safe. He made my feet like the feet of a deer, and set me secure on the heights.

—PSALM 18:28–33

A smooth sea never made a skillful mariner.

—ENGLISH PROVERB

What You Get Is What You See

Companies spend lots of money on consultants. These professionals come in from the outside, see how a firm docs business, determine how they could do better, and then tell the management what they see. Some employees might wonder why it's so important to listen to outsiders. Wouldn't people within the company have a better view? Not necessarily. Consultants have the gift of perspective. They see the big picture, evaluating the company in relation to their market, their potential market, and other companies.

You might think of God as our consultant. One of the most important gifts he gives us, especially in troubled times, is *perspective*. With the eye of faith, we can see what's truly going on, what's most important, and what needs to be done.

The prophet Elisha found himself a pawn in a border war between Israel and Syria. When he made some accurate prophecies that helped Israel in a few key battles, the king of Syria decided to capture him. He sent an army to do so. When Elisha's assistant looked out the window and saw enemy soldiers surrounding the town with their horses and chariots, he was scared stiff.

"Do not be afraid," the prophet said, "for there are more with us than there are with them." Then he asked God to "open the eyes" of his assistant "that he may see" (2 Kings 6:16–17). Suddenly the assistant saw that chariots of fire, God's own defense force, protected the town.

It's a helpful picture for us when we feel surrounded by trouble—whether it's terrorism, an environmental disaster, or an economic crisis. The trouble is not the whole picture. There are also invisible protective forces fighting for our bodies and souls. God does not abandon us.

This divine perspective helps us withstand the power of fear. When things start going wrong, we can easily become paralyzed with the fear that things will *keep* going wrong. Events are hurtling out of our control, and we expect the worst. But when those chariots of fire enter the picture, our view changes. We know that someone we trust is ultimately in control.

Our faith helps us see what's really going on—no more, no less. We don't deny the difficulty, but neither do we let fear compound the trouble.

Our faith helps us see what's really important. You might have lost money in the recent economic downturn, but how important is money in the grand scheme of things? We're not used to asking that question, but it's a good one. What is most important in this life of ours? Trying times often refocus our priorities.

Our faith helps us see what needs to be done. God gives a certain clarity of thought in times of crisis. Fear clouds our minds, but faith blows those clouds away. Todd Beamer, along with the other passengers on Flight 93, developed a plan that saved lives and inspired a nation. Likewise, God will give you the clarity of thought to see your own course of action.

Our lives are full of supposes. Suppose this should happen, or suppose that should happen; what could we do; how could we bear it? But, if we are living in the high tower of the dwelling place of God, all these supposes will drop out of our lives.

—HANNAH WHITALL SMITH

Dear Lord, when I'm paralyzed by what I can or cannot see with my human sight, remind me that there is an unseen realm over which you also preside. And with that reminder, by your grace at work in my entire being, I will unclench my fists, relax my jaw, let out a sigh of relief and release, and let my heart, soul, mind, and strength rest in you, trust you, and love you as it should. Father, I don't want to be faithless; I want to be faith-filled and faithful in keeping my focus on you. I want to be bold when boldness is required; I want to be gentle when that is what is needed; I want to act or wait, speak or be silent as your Spirit directs in each instance of life. Thank you for granting me eyes of faith to see from an eternal per-spective, from a perspective that knows you are always in control, no matter what things may look like in the here and now.

Now faith is the assurance of things hoped for, the conviction of things not seen. Indeed, by faith, our ancestors received approval. By faith we understand that the worlds were prepared by the word of God, so that what is seen was made from things that are not visible.... And without faith it is impossible to please God, for whoever would approach him must believe that he exists and that he rewards those who seek him.

—HEBREWS 11:1–3, 6

Courage, Control, and Compassion

The Lord also helps by giving us *courage* during a crisis. Not only do we see what needs to be done, but we also find the power to do it. The Holy Spirit gives us a push. "Be strong and courageous," the Lord told Joshua when he assumed command of the Israelites.

"Do not be frightened or dismayed, for the Lord your God is with you wherever you go" (Joshua 1:9). We might never have to go up against a terrorist or a criminal, but we might be called upon to step out in faith—taking a new job, caring for a sick friend, or investing time in ministry to people needier than we are. We can do all this because we are tapping into a power greater than our own. The Lord our God is with us wherever we go.

The Spirit also helps us exercise *self-control* even in critical times. This personal discipline can keep us from overreacting to bad situations in negative, unhelpful ways. Everyone else might panic in the face of terrorism or an epidemic, but we're still committed to living God's way. That means we won't turn against our neighbors. We won't respond with racial hatred. We won't put our own needs ahead of others'. We won't let the love of money determine our actions. The disciplined life of the believer provides balance in an unbalanced time.

God's way of living always involves *compassion,* and that's another gift God bestows in crisis. It's tempting to focus on our own problems, but we recognize that others are hurting, too. It's our responsibility to reach out to others with God's love.

The Bible talks about the "fruit of the Spirit" that grows in the heart of a believer—love, joy, peace, patience, kindness, generosity, faithfulness, gentleness, and self-control (see Galatians 5:22–23). These are valuable gifts in any time but especially in times of terror.

In 2001, terrorists in the Philippines kidnapped a missionary couple, Martin and Gracia Burnham, and held them for ransom. Over the next year, they were in dire circumstances—hungry, hurting, and fearful. At one point, Gracia complained to Martin, telling him that she saw only evil around her and asking him how she could have love, joy, and peace in such wicked circumstances.

He simply replied that they needed to ask the Holy Spirit.

Gracia reports, "We started begging God for love and joy and peace and patience and contentment. And you know what? He started giving it to us. It wasn't all the time, but we had days and weeks of contentment and peace. When everyone else was getting fed well, and we were getting hardly anything, somehow there was contentment there. I can't explain it. The Lord did it for us."

A difficult road still lay ahead for Gracia. In a rescue attempt, Martin was fatally shot, but she has gone on to tell a powerful story of faith and strength and how she learned so much about herself and God, during which the Lord transformed her into a different person.

The Lord moves in mysterious ways, sometimes through sorrow, but he keeps providing the fruit of love, joy, peace, and so on to those who need it most.

Be patient, therefore, beloved, until the coming of the Lord. The farmer waits for the precious crop from the earth, being patient with it until it receives the early and late rains. You must also be patient. Strengthen your hearts for the coming of the Lord is near. . . . As an example of suffering and patience, beloved, take the prophets who spoke in the name of the Lord. Indeed we call blessed those who showed endurance. You have heard of the endurance of Job, and you have seen the purpose of the Lord, how the Lord is compassionate and merciful.

—JAMES 5:7–8, 10–11

You call me to keep in step with your Spirit, Father in heaven, but often I stumble along the way. Thank you for your patient love that lifts me up time and again. How I need you to fill me with courage when I feel I might become lost in fear, disappointment, and sorrow! How I need a gift of compassion from you to be able to reach out and minister your love to others, whether they seem deserving of it or not! How I need your Spirit of self-control when my own unwise impulses try to rise up and take over! O, Spirit of the living God, take my hand once again and lead me forward along this path of life, I pray. May I keep in step with you today and demonstrate your ways to a world that needs to see the reality of your truth and love exemplified before them.

Endurance is the crowning quality,
And patience all the passion of great hearts.

—JAMES RUSSELL LOWELL, "COLUMBUS"

Hoping and Coping

Scripture tells us to place our hope in the Lord (see Psalm 131:3). The scriptural word *hope* is an interesting one. We water it down when we use it for wishful thinking: "I hope it won't rain tomorrow." In the Bible, however, *hope* has a much stronger sense of expectation. To put your hope in the Lord is to bank on the notion that he will go with you into the future, guiding and blessing you.

This is another great gift of God that bolsters us when it seems our world is falling apart. To put it simply, hope helps us cope. The bombardment of bad news in the headlines day after day can take its toll on the hardiest emotions. It saps our energy and dampens our will. If the planet is disintegrating, what's the use of doing anything? If terror lurks at every step, how can we ever leave our homes? We can easily sink into lethargic depression—except we know that's not the whole story. Because we know God has the future in his hands, we can move forward throughout each day. Because we *hope* in the Lord, we can cope with whatever comes our way.

The Book of Lamentations records the sorrow of the prophet Jeremiah after the defeat and destruction of Jerusalem. You can almost picture him wandering through the rubble—the stones of the once-glorious Temple and the walls that had crumbled before the Babylonian onslaught. "He has filled me with bitterness . . . , he has made my teeth grind on gravel, and made me cower in ashes; my soul is bereft of peace; I have forgotten what happiness is" (Lamentations 3:15–17). Maybe you can relate.

The prophet then has a turnaround. "This I call to mind, and therefore I have hope: The steadfast love of the Lord never ceases, his mercies never come to an end; they are new every morning; great is your faithfulness. 'The Lord is my portion,' says my soul, 'therefore I will hope in him.' The Lord is good to those who wait for him, to the soul that seeks him. It is good that one should wait quietly for the salvation of the Lord" (verses 21–26).

Morning by morning, God answers the world's bad news with his good news. He is faithful. He shows mercy. In this life and the next, he will help us, no matter what disaster threatens.

Dear Lord, I thank you for the mercies you bring to my life each day. Even in the midst of frightening situations, when I worry about my future or the well-being of those I love, you give me hope. You help me think clearly and avoid panic. You remind me that you have great plans for me, now and in the future, in this world and in the next. Too often I forget that you are still in charge, and your heart has a lot of room in it for me. Thank you for your daily love and support. I offer you my love and trust. Amen.

Chapter 3
DAILY WORK

This chapter focuses on "daily work." This doesn't just mean full-time salaried jobs. It's the cobbled-together schedule of the student or the domestic management of the homemaker. It might include volunteer commitments or hobbies or the never-ending task of parenting. What do you do each day? That's the question. As we go through our ordinary activities, we consistently need God's help. So how does God answer those prayers? How does he help us in our "daily work"?

Stupid Cricket!

A grad student was working on an important presentation, due the next day, worth half his semester grade. He knew he should have started earlier, but he was juggling a full-time job, a few other activities, and two graduate classes. There wasn't a lot of extra time in his schedule.

So now he was gearing up for an all-nighter. The only problem was that he was getting too old for that. Now in his 40s, he entered this grad program as a way to kick his career to a higher level. He was tired of his entry-level job with low pay and minimal responsibility. He wanted to make a difference and use his God-given talents. He was tired of driving an old car and living in a small, run-down apartment. He had felt God's guidance as he took a chance on going back to school. Now he needed God's help to pass this class.

Back in college, all-nighters were a part of the culture. Drink a gallon of coffee and crank up some loud music on headphones, and he could easily study through the wee hours. Now, however, he found his brain getting fuzzy around midnight. Caffeine did bad things to his system, so he avoided it. Even if he could stay awake all night, it would be difficult to come up with any brilliant ideas for the presentation. The situation was looking more and more hopeless as the clock ticked its way into the A.M.

So he prayed: *Lord, you led me here. Please help me now. Keep me awake and alert to do the work I need to do.*

There was no burst of energy in his body, just a solid resolve to keep working as long as he could. And things were going fairly well...except for that stupid cricket.

He had this problem before. A cricket would vault into his apartment and chirp all night. A year earlier he had spent a sleepless night overturning furniture, scouring corners, trying to find the chirping cricket and smash it, but those creatures are elusive. On this night of study he knew he couldn't waste any time hunting down the cricket, so it chirped away merrily as he kept working. Every chirp put him on edge, like a blaring car horn or an annoying alarm clock.

He complained to the Lord about it: *Why, on this night of all nights, did you let this insect into my apartment? I don't need this, Lord. This stupid cricket is going to keep me up all night.*

A pause. He thought about what he had just said. Maybe this cricket could keep him alert long enough for him to get his work done. He shook his head, smiled, and resumed his study. Energized by the chirping, he was able to prepare a successful presentation.

"Be careful what you pray for," it has been said. "You're liable to get it." The whole story might seem silly to you—it seemed silly to the grad student at the time—but it's a great illustration of an oft-quoted verse: "We know that all things work together for good, for those who love God, who are called according to his purpose" (Romans 8:28). This doesn't mean that all things *are* good. The cricket was still bothersome and the grad student's life was still stressful. This verse doesn't prescribe denial. But we're told that all things *work together* for good, according to God's purpose.

Some folks love to cite Romans 8:28 when tragic events occur, and it can be a great comfort. But we often see God spinning things together for good in the more mundane areas of our daily lives as well. Many times God chooses to use the irksome inconveniences of our day-to-day grind to help us while answering our prayers.

An inconvenience is only an adventure wrongly considered; an adventure is an inconvenience rightly considered.

—G. K. CHESTERTON, "ON RUNNING AFTER ONE'S HAT, ALL THINGS CONSIDERED"

Dear heavenly Father, I'm often so busy writing scripts for you—roles for you to play in answering my prayers—that I sometimes miss seeing your plan unfold as Lord of the universe. Instead, I jump to conclusions about what seems to me to be adversities and challenges. I don't consult with you; neither do I ask you to reveal your purpose to me nor grant me wisdom and insight in each of my experiences. Ah! Please help me grow today a little—perhaps even a lot—as I encounter obstacles in my life. May I stop and seek your direction as I try to interpret the puzzling events in my life. Thank you, Lord, for honoring me with a role in the bigger story of your eternal love at work in the world.

The human mind may devise many plans, but it is the purpose of the Lord that will be established.

—PROVERBS 19:21

The Bad Boss

You've had one. Everybody has. At least one, maybe more. The "bad boss." The person whose sole purpose in life is to give you a hard time. Whatever you do, it's not good enough. This "boss" might be a teacher, a coach, a regular customer, or an important client, but in any case they seem to care only about themselves and never about you. The bad boss gives you too much work, sets unrealistic deadlines, and claims credit for your ideas. You begin dreaming of the day when you can stand before your boss and say, "I quit."

Bad bosses inspire many prayers: *Lord, help me survive! Lord, change her so she's nicer! Lord, strike him down with a disease that will keep him out of work for a month!*

How does God answer these prayers? Sometimes (but rarely) by changing the boss. Often by changing the relationship. Usually by changing you.

For modern readers, one of the most difficult subjects to deal with in the Bible is slavery. Of course, we find it patently offensive that one person could own another, but it was a reality in the ancient world.

Surprisingly, the Bible doesn't speak out much against slavery. It seems to accept the situation and try to make the best of it. So if you think your boss is "a real slave driver," Scripture has a lot to tell you.

"Slaves, accept the authority of your masters with all deference," writes the Apostle Peter, "not only those who are kind and gentle but also those who are harsh" (1 Peter 2:18). Several other passages urge slaves to obey their masters while remembering that their ultimate master is God. That's important to remember when your boss asks you to work all weekend. You have a choice: Do it grudgingly for your boss or do it willingly for the Lord. So if you pray for God to help you with your daily work, he might just remind you that he's the one you're really working for.

As Peter continues his instruction to slaves, he assumes that some bosses/masters will treat their underlings unfairly. We need to endure and continue to work honestly and diligently. "For it is a credit to you if, being aware of God, you endure pain while suffering unjustly. If you endure when you are beaten for doing wrong, what credit is that? But if you endure when you do right and suffer for it, you have God's approval. For to this you have been called, because Christ also suffered for you, leaving you

an example, so that you should follow in his steps"
(1 Peter 2:19–21).

So if you call for God's help, he might give you
endurance. And he might give you a greater sense of
communion with Christ, who also endured extreme
mistreatment.

Lord God, I don't know how to stop enduring
my boss other than to grit my teeth. I don't
know how to change my perspective, even in
light of what your Word has revealed to me.
I need your help! I need you to grant me
grace to see you as the one I'm serving from
day to day. I need your mercy to flow through
me toward my boss. I know you see them
differently than I do. You see their deepest
insecurities, needs, sorrow, and bitterness—
whatever it is that's driving their abrasive-
ness. Remind me to pray for my boss during
the workday and then to entrust myself to
you for what I need to do to properly honor
them in a way that is pleasing to you.

Slaves, obey your earthly masters in everything, not only while being watched and in order to please them, but wholeheartedly, fearing the Lord. Whatever your task, put yourselves into it, as done for the Lord and not for your masters, since you know that from the Lord you will receive the inheritance as your reward; you serve the Lord Christ.

—COLOSSIANS 3:22–24

Company Politics

Sometimes it's not just the boss, but your coworkers who give you grief. Workplaces can bristle with gossip, grudges, and backstabbing. This climate makes many people hate to go to work each day.

You can ask God to change the people you work with, and that sort of miracle occasionally occurs, but it's far more likely that God will use *you* to transform the situation or that he will strengthen and comfort you as you attempt to deal with it.

The Apostle Paul gave some practical advice for getting along with others in less-than-ideal circumstances:

"Bless those who persecute you; bless and do not curse them" (Romans 12:14). This is not easy to do, but this is the power God gives us.

"Rejoice with those who rejoice, weep with those who weep" (verse 15). The Holy Spirit will help you make an emotional connection with your coworkers.

"Live in harmony with one another; do not be haughty, but associate with the lowly; do not claim to be wiser than you are" (verse 16). Sometimes we unwittingly contribute to the nasty climate in the workplace by adopting a superior attitude, perhaps even a holier-than-thou mind-set. God can help us by instilling humility into our character.

"Do not repay anyone evil for evil.... If it is possible, so far as it depends on you, live peaceably with all. Beloved, never avenge yourselves.... No, if your enemies are hungry, feed them; if they are thirsty, give them something to drink" (verses 17–20). The Lord will help us withstand attacks without retaliating. This is hard to do; it's not natural. But God's Spirit can help us turn the other cheek.

"Do not be overcome by evil, but overcome evil with good" (verse 21). Thus the miracle God works through you can transform your workplace.

⌢

Where do I begin, Lord? I've given up so much ground at times, participating in the ugly side of interpersonal strife at work. How do I begin shining the light of what is upright and good in a humble way, rather than a self-righteous one? I'll feel like (and maybe look like) a hypocrite. Do I need to make some amends or apologies? Grant me sincerity in my repentance, as well as wisdom in my steps. Keep me from falling back into old patterns, I pray, and cause me to tread carefully forward—following your Spirit's lead in promoting peace and harmony. Please use me from now on to help mend the broken and scattered pieces of teamwork and cooperation. For the glory of your name, I ask these things.

Do all things without murmuring and arguing, so that you may be blameless and innocent, children of God without blemish in the midst of a crooked and perverse generation, in which you shine like stars in the world.

—PHILIPPIANS 2:14–15

Nothing so completely baffles one who is full of trick and duplicity himself, than straightforward and simple integrity in another.

—CHARLES CALBE COLTON, *LACON*

Job Stress

Daniel ran a small business, selling specialty products to larger manufacturers. It had always been a dream of his to be his own boss. Of course, he soon realized that the independent supplier has 20 bosses or more.

Every client is a boss, making demands, establishing deadlines, and so on. At one point he realized that he hadn't really been happy for several months. The things he used to enjoy—family time, playing softball with the church team, and watching sports with his son and his friends—were now tinged with anxiety over his business. He happened to mention this at a meeting of his church men's group, and they prayed for him: *Lord, help Daniel deal with his work stress.*

In the following weeks, Daniel zeroed in on one particular client who was always giving him a hard time, changing specs and deadlines and never quite happy with the result. While this client was providing about 20 percent of his business, Daniel felt he was spending 50 percent of his time trying to satisfy him.

First, he met with the client and explained the problem. The man agreed to change, but he didn't. The next month saw more of the same treatment. So Daniel made a very difficult decision, severing ties with the troublesome client. "It just isn't worth it," he told a friend. "I don't know how I'm going to replace that income, but this guy is ruining my life. I can't let that happen anymore." After taking that step, he went through a time where money was tight, but he was smiling a lot more.

Stress is a part of life. If you had zero stress, you'd be dead. But we all have times when stress is especially difficult, and this often involves our daily work. There's often too much to do and too little time, or perhaps the working conditions are difficult, or we run up against unrealistic expectations.

When we ask God for help, he often does what he did for Daniel, providing the clarity of analysis and the courage he needed to make a tough decision that improved his situation. In some cases, God gives us the wisdom and discipline to take stress-reducing steps in other areas of life—sleeping or eating better, exercising, losing weight, and meditating on God's Word. But there's also an important question that God might bring to our minds: *How important is it to do all the things you're trying to do?*

Whether you're a homemaker trying to maintain a "perfect" home or a ladder-climbing executive trying to reach a higher pay scale, you might be worshipping a kind of idol—perfectionism, money, fame, personal accomplishment, or a particular relationship. These "false gods" put demands on you that can make you miserable. God helps us by targeting these idols and setting us free from them.

I just realized, my supreme Lord, that long periods of time go by during which I don't ever stop to ask what is driving me to do the things I do. Are you calling me aside to help me look at what I'm doing, and why I'm doing it? Thank you for interceding in my life, because sometimes I feel as if I'm on an out-of-control ride that I don't know how to stop. And because I'm in the thick of things, I don't have the perspective I need to make good choices about what is truly meaningful. Search for me here in the chaos, Lord, and lift me into the peace of your presence where I can hear you speak. Help me listen and be willing to let go of pet projects and precious "investments" I've made in one thing or another. It's all on the table, Lord. Does something—do a number of things—need to go?

Men for the sake of getting a living forget to live.
—MARGARET FULLER, *SUMMER ON THE LAKES*

Losing a Job

Nowadays, people worry about losing their jobs, and many others have lost them. The financial implications are considerable, and we'll deal with those in the next chapter. But there's also emotional fallout with job loss. Anxiety is high before and after the axe falls. And self-esteem usually takes a hit. Often there's anger toward the company or boss. There might also be spiritual questions, such as: *How could God let this happen?*

Nevertheless, God provides comfort and support in these difficult times. But he also has a strange way of redeeming such situations.

Janey worked as an editor for a publication that was losing subscribers. For about three years it was on the verge of collapse—an extremely anxious period for everyone—and then it finally went under. Janey was jobless. Interviewing for a half-dozen similar positions, she was always on the short list but never the final choice. Meanwhile, she took freelance writing jobs to make ends meet. Within a year, as she continued with one frustrating interview after another, she found that her freelance work was growing. She had always dreamed of working on her own as a writer, but she lacked the courage to do so. This dire situation had actually forced her into the job of her dreams.

So if you're smarting from the loss of a job, don't hesitate to call for God's help. Maybe he'll help you redefine the kind of work you do.

That you may lead lives worthy of the Lord, fully pleasing to him, as you bear fruit in every good work and as you grow in the knowledge of God. May you be made strong with all the strength that comes from his glorious power, and may you be prepared to endure everything with patience, while joyfully giving thanks to the Father, who has enabled you to share in the inheritance of the saints in the light.

—COLOSSIANS 1:10–12

Dear Lord, my days are filled
with work of one kind or
another. You know the
problems I face—drudgery
and drama, insecurity and stress.
My working relationships can
be difficult, too. I ask for your
help day after day. Make me the
kind of worker you want me to
be—loyal, cheerful, honest, and
diligent. Help me reflect your
love to the people I work with.
Give me creativity and
wisdom to meet the challenges
I face each day. And keep
reminding me that it's you for
whom I'm working.

Chapter 4

God Is My Cosigner

Finances had reached a point where a single mother needed to move her family to a cheaper apartment. The problem was, she didn't have the money to make the move. As she calculated the moving costs, they came to $1,000, which was about $1,000 more than she had to spend. She felt stuck.

Then a friend invited her to church. She figured it might cheer her up a little, and maybe she could pray for a miracle. The service moved her, and she even put the little money she had in the offering plate.

That's when a woman—a complete stranger—tapped her on the shoulder and said, "God has his eye on you." The woman handed her a check for $1,000.

The single mother was stunned. No one knew that this was the exact amount she needed. That was between her and God. She had not told her friend or anyone else at that church, but somehow God sent this benefactor to help her.

Skeptics might scoff, but this sort of thing happens far too often to be mere coincidence. Sometimes God miraculously provides exactly what we need when we need it. People pray, and suddenly an old friend decides to repay a forgotten loan or a distant aunt sends a belated birthday check. One struggling writer had to take a bus trip to see a needy friend, but he couldn't afford the ticket. Then he was paid for a book review he had sent off a year earlier—in the exact amount of the ticket price.

God does not always work such jaw-dropping, head-scratching miracles, but he certainly can and he sometimes chooses this method. It's a way to remind us that he's there and he cares.

Wonder Bread

Most people know the story of Moses parting the Red Sea so the Israelites could escape from Egypt. But then what? They found themselves in the Sinai Desert. The fertile land of the Nile Valley was left behind as they ventured into a land of rocky canyons. How would they find food? Some complained and insisted on going back to Egypt.

Despite their faithlessness, God worked a miracle for them, sending bread from the sky. People woke up one morning and discovered that the ground was covered with frostlike seed. "What is it?" they wondered. In Hebrew, the word for "what is it?" is *manna*.

This "wonder bread" was sweet to eat, but it spoiled quickly. They could gather as much as they wanted for the day, but it would spoil overnight. They couldn't hoard it or trade it. God wasn't making them rich; he was just meeting their needs.

That principle still applies as God meets our needs today. We might ask God to make us "financially secure," so we never have to worry about money ever again. But if we found security in our money, we wouldn't have to rely on God ever again. Why would God want to do that?

God is interested in providing timely help to meet our immediate needs, and sometimes these mini-miracles dazzle us, but there are other ways he helps our economic situations.

*"Money never made a man
happy yet, nor will it.
There is nothing in its nature to
produce happiness. The more
a man has, the more he wants."*

—BENJAMIN FRANKLIN

[Jesus said,] "I tell you, do not worry about your life, what you will eat or what you will drink, or about your body, what you will wear. Is not life more than food, and the body more than clothing? . . . Therefore do not worry, saying 'What will we eat?' or 'What will we drink?' or 'What will we wear?' For . . . indeed your heavenly Father knows that you need all these things. But strive first for the kingdom of God and his righteousness, and all these things will be given to you as well."

—MATTHEW 6:25, 31–33

Community

When Sherry and John left for work one day, they had no idea it was the last time they would see their treasured house. An electrical short-circuit sparked a fire that quickly destroyed their home. Word went out to the members of their church, who responded with food and clothing. Sherry and John were invited to use the church computers, phones, and copiers as they tried to rebuild their lives, negotiating with insurance adjusters and contractors. Yes, they lost a great deal in that fire. They still grieve the missing photo albums and mementos, but they gained something even greater: the love and support of the people of God.

If you're looking for a miracle, you might just find it in the warm smiles and loving embraces of others. If you're calling on God to act mightily to meet your needs, the answer often comes from God's people.

The Acts of the Apostles tells about the beginnings of Christianity, after Jesus ascended to heaven. On the wondrous day of Pentecost, the number of disciples exploded from 120 to more than 3,000. Many of these new converts were pilgrims in Jerusalem, travelers from other lands. When they decided to stay and learn about Jesus, many of them would be cut off from their homes and jobs, and some of their families even disowned them. But we're told that the believers cared for these needy newcomers. "They would sell their possessions and goods and distribute the proceeds to all, as any had need" (Acts 2:45). From the beginning of the church, Christians shared with those in need. It was in their spiritual DNA.

When Scripture talks about the "fellowship" of the early church, the Greek word is *koinonia*, or literally, "commonness." We're not talking about potlucks and softball games, though there's nothing wrong with that kind of fellowship. This is a different thing entirely. "No one claimed private ownership of any possessions, but everything they owned was held in common. . . . There was not a needy person among them, for as many as owned lands or houses sold them and brought the proceeds of what was sold" (Acts 4:32, 34). Some folks worry that this sounds like communism or socialism, but there's no *ism* involved. It's Christian love at work. If all that you own is a gift from God, and God asks you to love others, then it only makes sense to share your goods with those in need. And if you're the one in need, it's required of you to receive this support cheerfully and thankfully. Sherry and John will tell you that it wasn't easy at first to receive charity from their church friends, but they soon realized that this was God's way of helping them and that they needed to accept it.

Let love be genuine; hate what is evil, hold fast to what is good; love one another with mutual affection; outdo one another in showing honor. Do not lag in zeal, be ardent in spirit, serve the Lord. Rejoice in hope, be patient in suffering, persevere in prayer. Contribute to the needs of the saints; extend hospitality to strangers.

—ROMANS 12:9–13

Riches may enable us to confer favors, but to confer them with propriety and grace requires something riches cannot give.

—CHARLES CALEB COLTON, *LACON*

Ah, Lord! Sometimes the way you provide for me pinches my pride. I feel an obligation to provide for myself and not burden others with that responsibility. But in times of dire need, I see that it is a beneficial life lesson for me to receive your provision from your people, teaching me lessons in such things as humility, interdependence, gratitude, and love. And let me also see the need to be generous in the future. Help me to let go of any judgments I've held in my heart toward or against those who have sought and received benevolence in the past. That's another reason it's extremely difficult for me to accept help—those secret senses of personal superiority and of disdain for others who are in need. Thank you for shining your light on these dark places in my heart and mind. Cleanse me from such pride and prejudice, and bring my love for you and your people closer to completion through these trials. Amen.

Contentment

The brilliant British writer C. S. Lewis drew a helpful analogy that involves hotels and expectations. We'll paraphrase. Let's say you're going on vacation, and you make reservations at the Grand Hotel. You know nothing about this place in advance, but you expect it to be an economy lodging, a basic place to sleep with no amenities. Well, you get there and find it's a lot nicer than you expected. It's not the top of the line, as hotels go, but it's quite good. You're delightfully surprised.

Then over the complimentary continental breakfast the next morning, you strike up a conversation with another traveler who has nothing but complaints. It turns out this person was expecting a five-star hotel with the most luxurious accommodations. The Grand Hotel isn't nearly as grand as he expected, and he is upset about it.

Two travelers with identical rooms in the same hotel, but one is delighted while the other is upset. What's the difference? Only the expectations. Your neighbor feels he's entitled to much more luxury, while you're happy that you got this much.

When the national economy goes south, many people are forced to get by on much less money than they are accustomed. They're bothered that they have to cut their budget. They feel that God is mistreating them—*how could he let this happen?*

The fact is, however, that many people in this world would be delighted with that same amount of money. It's not the amount that's important; it's the expectations. We feel we're entitled to X amount of income, and we've built our lives around that number. When that number is reduced, we might ask God for help: *Please restore our fortunes!* He might answer that plea in an entirely different way. Instead of giving us more money, he might help us be satisfied with less.

"I have learned to be content with whatever I have," wrote the Apostle Paul to the Philippians. "I know what it is to have little, and I know what it is to have plenty. In any and all circumstances I have learned the secret of being well-fed and of going hungry, of having plenty and of being in need. I can do all things through him who strengthens me" (Philippians 4:11–13).

Maybe you've heard that last sentence—"I can do all things…"—quoted as a promise of God's empowerment, and it is. But it's worth noting that the context is *contentment*. Paul says he can deal with any circumstance, rich or poor, because God strengthens him in all situations.

By the way, he was in prison when he wrote this letter to the Philippians.

So if economic circumstances have imprisoned you, maybe God will help by enabling you to live contentedly within your new situation.

Of course, there is great gain in godliness combined with contentment; for we brought nothing into the world, so that we can take nothing out of it; but if we have food and clothing, we will be content with these. But those who want to be rich fall into temptation and are trapped by many senseless and harmful desires that plunge people into ruin and destruction. For the love of money is a root of all kinds of evil, and in their eagerness to be rich some have wandered away from the faith and pierced themselves with many pains.

—1 TIMOTHY 6:6–10

Dear Father in heaven, I need a true perspective that holds my focus when the glam and glitter around me try to turn my head. Help me see the things of this world as passing away, not truly invested with the value and worth others would try to make me believe they have. This week's fashion statement will be loathed in six months. This year's car model will be history next year. All that paraphernalia at the bookstore that I don't really need will end up gathering dust. Help me to not be impulsive, gullible, or driven by peer pressure or public opinion. I want to know true contentment that comes in being grateful for your provisions and okay with letting the things of the world pass me by.

The Blessing of Poverty

"I used to be a rising star," says Denise. "I had an executive position that others envied, and I pulled down a hefty salary. I oversaw the work of dozens, managing a multimillion-dollar budget. My husband and I had a big house in a ritzy suburb. We had everything we could ever want ... except happiness."

Denise had grown up in a household of faith, but she hadn't paid much attention to that as she climbed the corporate ladder. Yet the stress was now getting to her, her marriage was wearing thin, and there was a nagging sense of discontentment in her heart. That's when she got a call from a new church in town that was just starting up. It was as if God had phoned her personally. She knew this was something she had to get involved with. She knew it was time to reclaim her faith.

Over the next few years, Denise and her husband became very active in this new church, and she found her job was less and less important to her. Several years later, she sensed that God was calling her to minister to others full time. When she shared these thoughts with her husband, he was surprisingly supportive. She applied to a seminary and began pastoral training.

This meant a complete overhaul of their budget and a move to a cheaper home. It took some getting used to, but Denise says, "For the first time in a long time, I was truly happy. I knew I was where God wanted me to be." After completing seminary, Denise secured a church job, where she was able to help many others who were going through tough times. When the old church building was declared unsafe and had to be torn down, she led the people through a difficult transition, because she had been through a transition herself.

We keep saying, "Money can't buy happiness," but we don't really believe it, do we? We assume that money *can* purchase the things that bring us happiness, so when we lose money, we fear that we're doomed to a less fulfilling life.

Jesus, however, says just the opposite. "Blessed are you who are poor" (Luke 6:20). What was he thinking? Well, maybe he was saying that wealth distracts us from God. We tend to trust in our bank accounts rather than the Lord. When we're poor, we *have* to look to him for help.

A rich young man came to Jesus once and wanted to know the secret of eternal life. He had lived a good life, but he still felt something was missing. Jesus' response is a curious one that still challenges modern readers. "Sell all that you own and distribute the money to the poor..., then come, follow me." Rather than taking the challenge of becoming poor and learning to rely on God, the rich young man went away "sad; for he was very rich" (Luke 18:22–23).

Is Jesus telling us that we have to give away all our possessions? Maybe not, but he was teaching an important principle. The secret to eternal life is to *rely on God,* and when troubling circumstances come upon us, we draw closer to him. That's why the poor are blessed, because they get to trust God for everything.

So when you ask God for help in your time of economic upheaval, he might miraculously meet your financial needs, and he might do this by having Christian friends help you out. He might also teach you contentment, allowing you to lower your expectations. And he might give you the blessing of relying on him, holding your heart close to his as you keep asking him for daily bread.

Dear Lord, I lean on you now
in my time of need. You know the
circumstances that have brought
me to this point. You know exactly
what's my fault and what's not.
I want to move forward, and I need
your help. Please provide for my
needs, as you have promised to do.
Let me feel the embrace of the
community of faith. Help me be
content with less than what I'm
used to. Most of all, Lord, I ask that
you would draw me closer to you
in these challenging days. I want to
learn to rely on your grace. Amen.

Chapter 5
The Problem with Other People

Little Emma was painfully shy, so her parents were a bit nervous when they sent her off to a birthday party at a neighbor's house. When she came home, they asked for a full report. Was it nice? Did she have fun?

"Yeah, it was okay," Emma replied, "except for all those other people."

Many of us live our lives like that. We engage in our daily work; we do our errands; we go to church; hang out with friends . . . and it's "okay, except for all those other people." Relationships are difficult, whether they're casual or serious. In fact, the more intimate the connection, the more trouble we'll have. You can shrug off a slight from the clerk at the convenience store, but it's a big deal if your spouse or sibling annoys you.

We learn those difficulties early, growing up under the control of imperfect parents. Brothers and sisters tease and compete along the way. We find "best friends" who disappoint us at times, and we struggle through the minefield of adolescent romance, hurting and getting hurt. Many of us get married, entering relationships that are wonderful yet challenging, and there are often children who both delight us and cause anxiety. Well into adulthood, we develop meaningful bonds with coworkers, church folks, and Facebook friends, and we find the dynamics with our parents and children shifting through the years. With all of the above, we need God's help.

Certainly those close relationships with family and friends carry many blessings, but if you're looking for easy street, you have the wrong coordinates. As a rule, people don't do what you want them to do. In fact, they often do the very things you *don't* want. Intentionally or not, they irk you. We keep longing for the perfect relationship, but the reality of our interactions falls far short.

So how should we pray about these situations? How will God help us when we have problems with other people?

Lord, Change Them!

We can always ask God to change the other person. Our wishes may not come true, but it doesn't hurt to ask God.

As a sophomore in high school, Pete fell madly in love with a girl in his class named Janet. The problem was, she didn't seem to be quite as interested in him. Even at that age, Pete's faith was strong. He believed in miracles, and every night he prayed for one: "Lord, make Janet love me!"

He began walking with her part of the way home from school. They became good friends. She told him about other boys who expressed interest in her, which drove him crazy, but he tried to remain patient, waiting for the moment when God would work his miracle. "Please, Lord, I beg you, make Janet love me!"

A year-and-a-half went by, with no interest on Janet's part. Pete kept praying. "Dear, dear Lord, I'm burning with desire here. I want Janet to love me. If it be your will, Lord, please do *something*."

And then, on the walk home from school, Janet announced that her father had been transferred and she would soon be moving away.

Did God help Pete? Not in the way he wanted. Maybe the move was a way to free Pete from a misguided adolescent crush. Maybe the whole thing was a way to teach Pete patience. He certainly got into a habit of praying every night, always a good habit to develop. And at some point after the fact, Pete realized that he probably should have told Janet, and not just the Lord, about his feelings for her. That's an important lesson for a schoolboy to learn.

It might seem like a great display of faith to trust God to change someone's heart or their actions, but it's problematic on several counts. Usually it means we're requesting that God make others live the way *we* want them to, and who's to say we know what is the best way for them to live? You may know people who feel they have the right to tell everyone else what to do, and you don't want to be one of those people— nor should you expect God to help you do that.

Another factor is that God generally refrains from making people live the way *he* wants, and he certainly knows what's best. From the Garden of Eden, God has valued human freedom, and he allows people to make their own decisions—even though he has to endure the consequences.

One of the Bible's strangest stories involves the prophet Hosea, whom God ordered to marry a prostitute. It should come as no surprise that she was unfaithful to him, and Hosea grieved deeply, but his life became a kind of parable about the relationship between God and his people. "A spirit of prostitution leads them astray; they are unfaithful to their God" (Hosea 4:12, NIV). In other passages, too, the Bible portrays God as a jilted lover, longing for his people to return to him. He woos, he threatens, he whispers his promises, but he does not snap his fingers to magically change their hearts. He wants them to choose freely.

And that's the message for Pete and for anyone else who wants God to make someone love them, or make a boss appreciate them, or make a child obey, or make the bank manager consider them worthy of a mortgage. People are free to feel and to think the way they want, and that freedom is very important to God.

I know it's true, Lord God, that while you're in control of the big picture, you don't micromanage your creation in the sense of taking away our free will when our decisions are contrary to your ways. Sometimes I wish you would! But you are not a control freak. In fact, your self-control truly amazes me, particularly when you refrain from grabbing me by the collar and shaking me when I'm being stubborn. Yet, while you don't impose your will on my life, you do invite me to obey your will and abide in fellowship with you.

Help me follow your example when it comes to interacting with others. Grant me a self-control that does not insist that people see things the way I see them or that they do things my way. Above all, help me seek pathways to fellowship with them—of course, not condoning or facilitating anything that would be wrong in their choices—but finding ways to reach out to them with love, while inviting them to join me on your path of life.

God did not make others as I would have made them. God did not give them to me so that I could dominate and control them, but so that I might find the Creator by means of them.

—DIETRICH BONHOEFFER

Changing Us

When you were a kid, did you ever make one of those works of art in which you cut out different pieces and suspended them from a coat hanger? It was called a "mobile." Art teachers loved it because it was not just a picture on a wall but something that shifted and swirled with constant energy. Tap just one piece of a mobile and the whole thing moves.

Child psychologists have used mobiles to explain how families work. Everyone is interconnected. If one member suffers, it affects everyone else. And we might say the same thing for all our relationships. They are *interactive*. You could sit around waiting for God to miraculously change someone, but you might get better results if you changed something about yourself or the situation. That might send this mobile spinning, and it might achieve the effect you want—or something even better.

So if you're asking God to improve a relationship you have, you've already taken the initial steps—that is, recognizing that something needs improvement and seeking assistance from our "very present help in trouble." But stop assuming that God just needs to zap the other person. Open yourself up to the positive changes God wants to make in you. And you do that by...

Listening.

"Let everyone be quick to listen, slow to speak, slow to anger," the Bible says, "for your anger does not produce God's righteousness" (James 1:19–20). Note the connection between listening and anger. You might be burning with righteous indignation, but hold your tongue and open your ears. You need to understand where the other person is coming from. Too often we assume that we are speaking on God's behalf when we scold others. We're just trying to make them more righteous, right? That's a good thing, right? Well, James says we need to listen first.

The truth is that, while God has plenty of reasons to express his righteous indignation, even he holds back on that in order to listen to us.

Could better listening transform a difficult relationship for you? Maybe. One of the major warning signs of marital trouble is when the partners stop listening to each other. One of the greatest gifts a parent can give a child is to turn off the TV, ignore the phone, and truly listen. Come to think of it, that's a pretty good gift for a child to give a parent, especially in the teenage years, when texting, touch screens, and video games tend to capture attention. Imagine the connection that could be made in just a half-hour of undistracted listening.

Of course, it's not just a matter of opening your ears. You need to open your mind and your heart as well. Counselors talk about the value of *active listening*—repeating key phrases after you hear them and asking questions to clarify what you've heard. This lets the other person know that you care, that you're following, and that you're truly listening and not just waiting for your turn to talk.

But what if you don't care? What if your friend/child/parent/spouse is kind of boring? Well, that's where you need God's help. "Let each of you look not to your own interests," writes the Apostle Paul, "but to the interests of others" (Philippians 2:4). You might be praying, "Lord, make this person more interesting." But according to this verse, a better prayer might be, "Lord, make me more interested."

Dear heavenly Father, it's been said that you gave us two ears and one mouth for a reason: to listen at least twice as much as we talk. Whether that was your purpose or not for making people the way you did, the idea is a good one. But it takes special grace to refrain from talking when what I'm hearing doesn't agree with me or I don't agree with it. Even when I do agree, I often feel so eager to share my perspective that I don't hear the other person out. Please forgive me for being selfish and even disobedient in my interaction with others. By your grace at work in my heart and mind, help me be quick to listen, slow to speak, and slow to anger, as your Word tells us to be. Amen.

Being selfless.

In the verse before the one just quoted, Paul wrote, "Do nothing from selfish ambition or conceit, but in humility regard others as better than yourselves" (Philippians 2:3). Before we hear the self-esteem police blowing their whistles, let's consider what this really means. Should we consider ourselves losers, worms, and unworthy of friendship? Of course not. But in relationships it helps when we treat others as if they were more important. Ideally, they're treating us that way too.

The following verses help to spell this out, using the example of Jesus, "who, though he was in the form of God, did not regard equality with God as something to be exploited, but emptied himself, taking the form of a slave" (Philippians 2:6–7). *Exploited* is a pretty good rendering of the Greek word that literally means *grabbed* or *grasped.* Jesus was certainly not a loser, but he didn't cling tightly to his equality with God. Instead, in humility, he became human, and a servile human at that. In the same way, we can feel really good about who we are—created by God, redeemed by Jesus, and gifted by the Holy Spirit. Each of us has much to offer, but as we seek to conduct our relationships, we must not cling to those things, as if we're better than anyone else. Instead, like Jesus, we must seek to serve others humbly.

That plays out in a lot of practical ways, from "What do you want to eat?" to "Who's washing the dishes?" to "Who's going to win this argument?" The closer the relationship, the more tightly the lives are inter-twined, and the more frequently these questions arise. When a marriage becomes contentious, or when children and parents are at odds, every day can be a war, with battles going on every few minutes. You might be praying, "Lord, help them see that I'm right!" But the more powerful prayer might be "Lord, help me give in, stop grasping my rights, and look for ways to serve."

Love is patient; love is kind; love is not envious or boastful or arrogant or rude. It does not insist on its own way; it is not irritable or resentful; it does not rejoice in wrongdoing, but rejoices in the truth. It bears all things, believes all things, hopes all things, endures all things.

—1 CORINTHIANS 13:4–7

Lord God, I'm not really inclined to
be humble and selfless. That's why
I need your saving grace at work in
my life, helping me keep in step with
your Holy Spirit. Thank you for Jesus'
example of humility. He came in the
flesh and humbled himself even to a
shameful kind of death, one reserved
for criminals. But as for myself,
I struggle to lay down my pride to
apologize for something I really *did*
do wrong. O Lord, have mercy on me
and help me lay down my selfishness
and take up the daily cross
of sacrificial love for others!

Having a vision.

Sometimes we fail to see the value in people. We
write them off, even though God might want to use
them in our lives.

As a college student, Rich got involved with a local church, helping out with its high-school youth group. Andrew, the youth leader, who was hired part-time by the church, took an instant liking to Rich, seeing him as not only a valuable teammate in ministry but also as someone who could become a good friend. Unfortunately, Rich didn't feel the same way. Andrew was sort of loud and kind of crude, not the type of friend Rich would choose. He already had plenty of pals at college; he didn't need another one. So when Andrew wanted to come over to campus and hang out, Rich was less than excited. Yet, over the next few years, through Andrew's sheer persistence, a genuine friendship developed. Rich began to see past the uncouth exterior and find a guy who was quite intelligent and fiercely loyal. He traded in his judgment for acceptance, and ultimately, appreciation. Looking back years later, Rich saw that he had learned a great deal from this unlikely friend.

The New Testament gives us a sketchy story involving Paul and Barnabas and a young associate named Mark. All three started out together on their first missionary journey, but Mark bailed out at one point. The reason is unclear. Homesickness or perhaps a run-in with Paul. In any case, as they prepared for a second mission trip, Barnabas wanted to take Mark again, but Paul refused. The disagreement was so strong that the two missionary friends split up—both physically and emotionally.

What kind of prayers do you think the three of them were praying about this? *Lord, show them how wrong he is?* We do have a number of prayers that Paul was praying for various churches, and we know he asked God to give the Ephesians a "spirit of wisdom and revelation as you come to know him, so that, with the eyes of your hearts enlightened, you may know what is the hope to which he has called you" (Ephesians 1:17–18).

Perhaps Paul had some sort of enlightenment in his heart. Maybe he began to see the "hope" to which God was calling Mark. In any case, toward the end of his life, he writes to another young protégé, Timothy, "Get Mark, and bring him with you, for he is useful in my ministry" (2 Timothy 4:11).

Is there someone you have given up hope on? Maybe you could ask God to enlighten the eyes of your heart and see if there's some hope left.

I judge too quickly, Father in heaven. I look at an appearance and draw a conclusion. I talk with a person once and think I know what they're about. Someone has a bad day and steps on my toes, and I write them off. I think I know where my spouse is heading with a comment, and I roll my eyes. Such things shouldn't have any place in my life, Lord! What do I do? I want to stop jumping to conclusions and give people grace and space to grow, even just to be themselves without withdrawing my love and acceptance. I'm flawed and need that same kind of grace from others. Please help me do to others as I would want them to do to me. Bring radical change to my heart and mind even now. In Jesus' sacred name, I ask. Amen.

Being courageous.

Sometimes a relationship just needs to change, big time. It's beyond tweaking. You can try to listen more or to be kinder, but there's a fundamental problem in the way things are. In such cases, you need the courage to change things drastically.

Dinah had such a situation with her husband, Charlie, who had been having affairs almost constantly in the ten years of their marriage. Wanting to be a loyal wife, she had put up with it, accepting him back each time he tearfully confessed and privately wondering why she wasn't good enough to hold his interest. But recently she had established some good friendships with women who supported her and built up her self-esteem. She also was taking the first steps on a spiritual journey, getting to know God again. All of this was steadily convincing her that her marriage was not really a marriage at all. Timidly she asked God to help her, though she wasn't sure what help she needed.

Charlie began packing for a weekend trip, saying that it was for work, but Dinah knew very well he was going to see his latest mistress. She's still not sure how she summoned the courage, but she said what needed to be said. "If you're going to see her, Charlie, then don't come back. Don't get me wrong: I'm not kicking you out. I want you to be married to me, but if you are, then it's me and only me. I'm not going to share you. That's what a marriage is, just you and me. If that's what you want, then stay here and be married to me. But if you need to go to her, then you don't have a home here anymore."

He left. She stood her ground and wouldn't take him back. The divorce was painful for her, but she saw it as a deliverance from a phony marriage. That relationship had to change, one way or the other, and God gave her the courage to change it.

Please don't take this as a recommendation for divorce. That's generally a sad option in a bad situation. The point is that there are often relationships that need major adjustments, and God might help you by offering the courage to make the necessary changes. You might have friendships that have degenerated into gossip or cynicism. Try to change course. Perhaps your marriage is beginning to sink into complacency, partners taking each other for granted. Step up and say something—get some counseling and look for new ways to reclaim love. Maybe your whole family is bickering, lying, or complaining, and you need to set up some drastically different patterns. Don't play the blame game. Let everyone take responsibility for setting a new tone.

And ask God for the courage to make that happen.

Dear Lord, today I bring before you my family, mentioning each member by name:_____. I ask you to bless each one. Become a major force in their lives, empowering them and enriching them with your presence.

I also pray for my closest friends, mentioning each one by name:_____. Use me to bless them, and use them to make me the person you want me to be.

Teach me more about love. It's an easy word to say, but it's a hard thing to do. Show me how to treat others as I want to be treated. Show me how to put others first. Show me how to see how valuable they are in your eyes. Amen.

Chapter 6

Doubt, Guilt, Anger, and Worry

They weren't the best of siblings. For most of their adult years, Ben and Patsy had a relationship that consisted solely of Christmas cards, and they even missed a few of those. Then they both had kids, and that gave them a reason to try to stay in touch. Still Patsy was surprised when Ben called to say that his daughter was sick with a serious fever.

"We thought that maybe you could say a prayer for her or something," Ben said.

"Me?"

"Well, you know. You're religious."

It was true. In fact, that had been one reason why the siblings had grown apart. Patsy was a devout Christian and, in fact, had gone to seminary to prepare for church ministry. She served her church in various capacities. Ben, on the other hand, had no interest in

God. He wasn't a confirmed atheist; it was just an area of life he didn't care about. He was too busy building a career, finding a wife, and raising a family.

"No," Patsy replied.

There was a moment of silence on the line.

"What? You're not going to pray for her?"

Patsy enjoyed her brother's reaction for a moment. "Oh, of course I'll pray for her. I do every day. But why don't you?"

"What?"

"Why don't you pray for her, Ben? It sounds as though you're asking me to do it so you don't have to pray."

"Well, I just thought that . . . it always seemed that you had a kind of 'in' with God. I think he would listen to your prayers more."

"I'm not sure about that, Ben. He hears my prayers all the time. But who would you rather hear from: Someone you talk to every day or someone you haven't heard from for years? I will certainly pray about this, but don't let me do it all for you. I think God would love to hear from you personally."

"Maybe I will."

There are many people in this world like Ben. Maybe you're one of them. These people tend to have a distant respect for God. They feel a need to turn to him in emergencies, but he's not at all involved in their daily lives. Religion is a foreign language to them. Sometimes, like Ben, they turn to religious folks they know in order to get a sort of recommendation. "Put in a good word for me with the Almighty, will you?"

There are numerous reasons why people feel they are unable to make a connection with God. Some people **doubt** that God would want to do them any favors. In some cases they consider it hypocritical, or inconsistent, to pray to God when they're not completely sure there is one. While there's something inside them that longs to cry out to a higher power for help, they don't know how to process that feeling. More likely, they feel **guilt** about certain behaviors that don't meet God's standards. Surely God wouldn't answer prayers from those in such poor moral condition, would he? And then some people are **angry** with God for certain tragedies he has allowed. As a result, they're giving him the silent treatment. Still others **worry** that there's some special style of prayer that God requires, and they don't know what that style is.

So let's consider doubt, guilt, anger, and worry. Will God help us deal with them? Will he provide the help we need despite these hurdles? If so, how?

Doubt

A man once came to Jesus in desperate straits, crying out that an evil spirit possessed his son. In fact, the boy displayed the frightening symptoms of what we now call "epilepsy"—suffering fits where he was unable to speak, dropping to the ground, foaming at the mouth, grinding his teeth, and becoming rigid. The father had brought his son to Jesus' disciples, but they were unable to help. Now he came before Jesus and begged, "If you are able to do anything, have pity on us and help us" (Mark 9:22).

It almost seems that Jesus chuckled a little as he repeats the man's phrase: "If you are able!" (verse 23). By this time, Jesus already had a reputation as an effective healer, but he doesn't focus on his own power, but rather on the man's faith. He adds, "All things can be done for the one who believes" (verse 23).

Responding to Jesus' words, the father cries out, "I believe; help my unbelief!" (verse 24). Jesus then proceeded to heal the boy.

Let's circle back on the father's statement. "I believe; help my unbelief!" Isn't that where we all find ourselves, standing on the corner of Belief and Unbelief? Flip through the Book of Psalms, and you'll spend a lot of time on this corner. You will find some amazing expressions of trust in God, as well as some deep doubts—"My God, my God, why have you forsaken me? Why are you so far from helping me?" (Psalm 22:1). If you think your doubts disqualify you from God's favor, you've missed the point.

Yes, Scripture indicates that our faith makes things happen, but not because we've shown ourselves worthy of God's help by the strength of our faith. It's merely because our faith clears the way for God to work. Faith is an electrical cord plugged into the wall. The power comes from far beyond us; our faith merely channels it.

In fact, the story of the believing/unbelieving father implies that Jesus' disciples were trying to heal the boy in their own power. When they wonder why they were ineffective, Jesus says, "This kind [of spirit] can come out only through prayer" (Mark 9:29). Perhaps they were relying only on their faith to try to achieve this healing, but apparently they weren't asking God for help. It's as if they had a beautiful new electrical cord but forgot to plug it in.

Jesus mentioned once that merely a tiny seed of faith could move mountains (see Matthew 17:20). That's poetic language; don't go trying to relocate Mount Everest. But the point is, it's not the size of our faith, but the object of it. That father was really at the perfect place, kneeling before the miracle-worker, saying he had some faith but not enough to achieve anything on his own. If you're struggling with some hybrid of faith and nonfaith, don't let that keep you from asking for help. The very fact that you're asking demonstrates all the faith you need.

It's a good thing to have all the props pulled out from under us occasionally. It gives us some sense of what is rock under our feet, and what is sand.

—MADELEINE L'ENGLE

When I struggle with doubt, O God, it's
not so much that I doubt you—though
I'll admit, at times, I do that—it's much
more about doubting myself: I doubt I'm
coming to you in the right way; I doubt
I'm saying the right words; I doubt I
deserve to be heard by you. So many
doubts! How do I get past them so I can
again talk with you openly about what is
important in my heart? Please help me
pray. Please help me trust that you want
to hear from me. Please help me not be
so unnerved by my inexperience and
feelings of inability. I feel the need
to talk with you, God.

Guilt

You might say there was a culture war going on in
first-century Israel. On one side were the devout

religious folks who prayed often, went regularly to the Temple, and tried hard to keep God's law while teaching others to do the same. On the other side were the compromisers, the backsliders, the traitors—those who had given up on the traditional faith and who had adopted the culture of the occupying Romans.

Guess which side Jesus hung out with?

He told a story about two men, one from each side of this divide, who went to the Temple to pray. One of them, a religious Pharisee, trumpeted his righteous behavior and expected God to be impressed. The other was a tax collector, known for swindling and an immoral lifestyle, including collaboration with the Romans. Jesus said that this man, "standing far off, would not even look up to heaven, but was beating his breast and saying, 'God, be merciful to me, a sinner!' I tell you, this man went down to his home justified rather than the other; for all who exalt themselves will be humbled, but all who humble themselves will be exalted" (Luke 18:13–14).

Imagine how Jesus' listeners reacted. How could he praise the backslider and condemn the Pharisee? Was he anti-religion? Didn't he like righteousness?

Was he pro-sin? Maybe this story raises similar questions for you. What if the same story were told today about a TV preacher and a drug dealer? It's a shocking story with a shocking conclusion.

The centerpiece of the story is the tax collector's prayer. We can say quite confidently that Jesus wasn't crazy about the tax collector's swindling or immorality, but this, he says, is the way to pray. When you come before God, don't puff up your proud heart with boasts about your religious activities. Own up to your sins and ask for mercy. That's how to be "justified," by counting on God's righteousness rather than your own.

Nowadays there are many who feel shut out of religion. They know their behavior has been far from righteous, and they don't expect to change anytime soon. Still, they wish they had a relationship with God, and every so often they try to pray, but they're not sure they're doing it right. When something goes wrong, they want to call out for God's help, but they know that God doesn't owe them anything. They figure they're not the sort of people who get their prayers answered.

Jesus says they're wrong. They're exactly the kind of people who get their prayers answered. They are in the perfect position to receive God's mercy, because that's what mercy is. To use a legal analogy, you don't "throw yourself on the mercy of the court" if you've declared yourself "not guilty." Mercy goes to those who know they don't deserve it.

So don't keep yourself from asking for God's help because you feel guilty. Throw yourself on his mercy. You can start with the tax collector's timid prayer: "God, be merciful to me, a sinner."

Here is a trustworthy saying that deserves full acceptance: Christ Jesus came into the world to save sinners—of whom I am the worst. But for that very reason I was shown mercy so that in me, the worst of sinners, Christ Jesus might display his unlimited patience as an example for those who would believe on him and receive eternal life.

—1 TIMOTHY 1:15–16 (NIV)

It's odd, my Lord, that when I think of "praying people," I think of them as "good" people or "perfect" people. But if that were the case, why would such people need to pray? Prayer is for seeking you out and for looking to you for help, strength, support, and forgiveness. And it occurs to me that there are no perfect people. Maybe I've been wrong. Perhaps those praying people are not self-righteous but are simply, by their prayers, admitting their need for you. Maybe they pray because they know they are messed up and not "good" or "perfect." Maybe it's time for me to begin praying and to stop worrying about not being good enough.

Anger

When her 25-year-old son committed suicide, Diane didn't know what to do. There had been no warning, just the shock and the lasting pain. She had been a faithful churchgoer all her life, but now it seemed God had done a terrible thing to her, so she decided to cut off ties with him. Diane stopped going to church, stopped praying, and stopped reading the Bible. What good was all of this religious devotion if God was going to take away what was most precious to her?

This reaction is more common than you might think. One question that touches many people deeply is How can God let tragedies happen? Even when we sort that out logically, we still have emotional troubles with it. We feel betrayed by God. After all we've done for him, how can he treat us so cruelly?

One elderly woman who had lived a very difficult life used to spit in disgust when anyone in her home mentioned God. "God, he doesn't exist," she would mutter. Then her granddaughter, a Christian, asked, "How can you be so angry with someone who doesn't exist?" In her innocent way, she touched on an important point. If God doesn't exist, there's no one to be angry with. The only reason to be angry is that we feel a living, active God is responsible for our mistreatment. And if God is living and active, then we need to deal with him, like it or not. He might not be acting the way we want him to, but he is acting.

So don't cloak your emotional response as a logical deduction. If it's an emotional issue, confront it as an emotional issue. Be honest about your feelings and talk them out. Don't withdraw. Don't throw tantrums. Don't cover it over until it emerges later in self-destructive behavior.

What if you're angry with your spouse or your best friend? How do you work through that? Well, many people go through the emotional withdrawal, tantrums, or passive-aggression, but the healthiest way is to confront it. "I'm upset with you and here's why."

Why can't you do the same thing with God?

Some folks feel that it's somehow sacrilegious to be angry with God. Even if they feel so hurt that they have disavowed their faith, they'd never dream of scolding God for what he's done to them. And yet that's exactly what we find in Scripture from some of its most prominent figures. Moses vehemently complained to God. So did David and the other psalmists. Jeremiah similarly pounded on heaven's door. "O Lord," cried the prophet Habakkuk, "how long shall I cry for help and you will not listen?... Why do you make me see wrongdoing and look at trouble? Destruction and violence are before me... and justice never prevails." He wonders how God can remain passive as he watches "the wicked swallow those more righteous than they." God has some explaining to do. The prophet Habakkuk says he'll climb up his watchtower and wait for a response. "I will keep watch to see what he will say to me, and what he will answer concerning my complaint" (Habakkuk 1:2–4, 13; 2:1).

Anger with God is not a deal-breaker. If these biblical believers can express their anger toward God and work through it, so can we. The key is communication. Come before God and let him know how you feel. Talk and listen. You don't need to be any more trusting than you are. Present your emotions in all their raw authenticity and, if you dare, ask for his help in healing them.

After her son's suicide, Diane shut herself off from all godly pursuits, but after several years of this protest, she felt a deep emptiness within. Her spirit was shriveling. That part of her that connected with God was shrinking from disuse. She began to realize that she had rejected her best means of support just when she needed it most. It wasn't easy to come back, and she had some knock-down-drag-out arguments with God along the way, but slowly he helped her find her way back to an active faith.

There is much pain that is quite noiseless; and vibrations that make human agonies are often a mere whisper in the roar of hurrying existence. There are glances of hatred that stab and raise no cry of murder; robberies that leave man or woman for ever beggared of peace and joy, yet kept secret by the sufferer—committed to no sound except that of low moans in the night, seen in no writing except that made on the face by the slow months of suppressed anguish and early morning tears. Many an inherited sorrow that has marred a life has been breathed into no human ear.

—GEORGE ELIOT

I can't understand, dear heavenly Father, why you let some things in life happen when you have the power and ability to intervene. I just don't understand. And it hurts to have the reality of that mystery hit so close to home. How do I keep trusting in you, when I feel betrayed by you? How do I keep the door of my heart open to you, when it feels as though you've slammed shut the door of help and hope in my face? Why, when I was waiting for you, did you not seem to show up? I feel caught between two dreadful options: The first is moving on with you, and the second is moving on without you. Both seem impossible right now, but I'm told that in time healing will come and you will still be here with me. I believe it's true; I just don't know how to get there from here. My soul is so bitter right now. Help me!

Worry

Perhaps you know some macho man who has no fear staring down a grizzly bear in a forest, but when a spider crawls up his leg, he whimpers. That's sort of what we see now. Doubt, guilt, and anger with God are huge spiritual and emotional issues, but the one that may derail our faith is the smallest and most common of problems—simple worrying.

A number of devout believers get sidetracked every day fretting about things that could go wrong. Mothers worry when their teenage children go out driving. Workers worry that the hours needed on a new project might eat into their weekend plans. Students worry that a subpar grade might keep them from acceptance at the college of their choice. You could certainly add some of your favorite worries.

One common response to worrying is positive thinking. "Why worry? Nothing bad will happen. You'll be fine." But this isn't necessarily true. In actuality, any of those worried-about things could happen.

During a fierce storm, a group of men on the Sea of Galilee considered it quite likely that their boat would go under. They woke Jesus with the charge:

"Teacher, do you not care that we are perishing?" (Mark 4:38). This wasn't just anxiety, it was out-and-out terror, but their question displayed a big problem with any sort of fear or worry. We assume the Lord doesn't care, when he does. "Cast all your anxiety on him," one of those fishermen wrote decades later, "because he cares for you" (1 Peter 5:7).

A second problem is that worrying does no good. "Can any of you by worrying add a single hour to your span of life?" asked Jesus (Matthew 6:27). In fact, modern research has shown that anxiety-based stress can subtract days and years from our lives. From a spiritual perspective, worry distracts us from more important pursuits. Jesus went on to say, "Therefore do not worry, saying, 'What will we eat?' or 'What will we drink?' or 'What will we wear?' . . . But strive first for the kingdom of God and his righteousness, and all these things [food, clothing] will be given to you as well" (Matthew 6:31, 33). Instead of fretting, consider what God might be planning, and how you can most effectively serve him.

Third, our worry keeps us from counting on God for help when we need it. "Do not worry about anything," Paul wrote to the Christians in Philippi, "but in everything by prayer and supplication with thanksgiving let your requests be made known to God. And the peace of God, which surpasses all understanding, will guard your hearts and your minds in Christ Jesus" (Philippians 4:6–7).

Those troubling scenarios that worry brings to your mind, bring them to God and leave them with him. Ask for his help to move past the anxiety and into the transforming power of his grace, which brings true inner peace.

Dear Lord, you know the spiritual issues that plague me. It's amazing to me that you'd even want to hear my prayer. I'm far from perfect, and I'm afraid my struggles make me not the kind of person you want knocking on your door, but here I am. So let's talk. I'm going to be brutally honest about my feelings and my questions. If there are things I need to be forgiven for, and I'm sure there are, let's talk about them. But honestly, I need to hear you explain what your plans are for me because there's a lot I don't understand. In any case, I'm ready to listen.

Chapter 7

DOES ANYBODY CARE?

She tried to put the best face on it. Freedom. After two years of dating a guy who wouldn't commit, she finally gave him an ultimatum. And he ran like a frightened squirrel out of her life. There. She had been delivered from the Great Hesitator. Mr. Wishy-Washy had left the building, and she was fortunate to be rid of him. Sure, he was cute...and nice...and funny...and they kind of fit together when he put his arm around her...but she would have waited a decade before he popped the question. It was better not to waste any more time. Get going when the going is good. She was free.

Free to spend another Saturday night by herself. Free to rent a video, pop some popcorn, and submerge herself in a private pity party. All her girlfriends were out with their boyfriends. She could call her mom, but that would be a bit like eating the chocolate brownies she just bought. It would feel good in the moment, but ultimately it would just make her more depressed.

She was 37 and, she thought, not a hot prospect. She had some success in her career, but that success had taken time away from relationship-building. And it seemed as though all the men she met at work were married, gay, or—just like her ex—commitment-phobic. Her biological clock was ticking so loudly that it kept her up at night. Was she destined for a life of solitude—no soul-mate, no lifetime partner, no pitter-patter of little feet?

"I'm lonely," she said out loud, and then it struck her funny that she was talking to herself. Appropriate. If a single woman goes crazy in a forest, is there anyone to hear her cries? No, she wasn't crazy...yet. Just really, really sad. She had just chased away the man she had hoped would love her forever, and now her heart was in tatters, her self-esteem was flatlining, and she wondered if there was anyone in the wide world who cared for her at all.

So she decided to do something drastic. She prayed.

David's Prayers of Anguish

"The Lord is near to the brokenhearted, and saves the crushed in spirit" (Psalm 34:18). According to ancient tradition, David wrote those words at an extremely difficult and confusing time in his life. As a young man, he had been hailed as a hero of Israel, the giant-killer, and he was welcomed into the royal court as a musician and companion to King Saul. He then married the king's daughter and became part of the royal family, but Saul soon turned against him. On a murderous rampage, the king hunted David through caves and canyons. Feeling beleaguered and betrayed, David wrote some psalms to relate what ordeals he was experiencing. In fact, his emotions were all over the place.

At one point his situation became so dangerous in Israel that he took shelter in enemy territory with the Philistines. (You might recall that it was a Philistine giant he had killed.) But David pretended to be insane so the Philistine king wouldn't feel threatened. Even that didn't work. The Philistine king essentially said, "I already have enough madmen around here; send him away" (see 1 Samuel 21).

We might wonder about David's actual sanity at this point. Saul had killed his friends, annulled his marriage, and sullied his reputation. David's most brilliant ploys were failing. He was bringing hardship on everyone he came in contact with, and no one understood exactly what he was going through.

Except, of course, the Lord.

All of this emotional turmoil served as inspiration for one of David's most hopeful psalms. "O taste and see that the Lord is good," he wrote. "Happy are those who take refuge in him" (Psalm 34:8).

How did David get from point A to point B? And how can we take that same journey? How does God help us when we're emotionally fried?

Blessed be the God and Father of our Lord Jesus Christ! By his great mercy he has given us a new birth into a living hope.... In this you rejoice, even if now for a little while you have had to suffer various trials so that the genuineness of

your faith—being more precious than gold that, though perishable, is tested by fire—may be found to result in praise and glory and honor when Jesus Christ is revealed.

—1 PETER 1:3, 6–7

Thank you, Lord, for all the instances in your Word that reveal people's emotional struggles. I'm so glad that you don't scold and shame us when we are sad; rather, you come alongside us and seek to encourage us. Thank you for remembering that we're mortals—"mere dust"—and susceptible to bouts of turmoil in our hearts. Thank you for the provisions you bring for lifting our spirits: prayer, Scripture, fellowship with others, nature, pets, and so many other blessings. Most of all, thank you for your own presence and for your Spirit, who sees us through our emotional struggles and heals our hearts.

Emotional healing is almost always a process. It takes time. There is a very important reason for this. Our heavenly Father is not only wanting to free us from the pain of past wounds, he is also desirous of bringing us into maturity, both spiritually and emotionally. That takes time, because we need time to learn to make the right choices. He loves us enough to take the months and years necessary to not only heal our wounds, but also build our character. Without growth of character we will get wounded again.

—FLOYD MCCLUNG,
THE COMPASSIONATE FATHER

Loneliness

Throughout the Bible's first chapter, at each stage of Creation, God declares his handiwork "good." The second chapter retells the story of Creation with special emphasis on the first man, Adam, and suddenly we see something that's "not good." After creating Adam, God says, "It is not good that the man should be alone" (Genesis 2:18). So God created the first woman, Eve.

Some might take this as an affirmation of marriage, but we can also see it as something larger. It is essential for us to be in relationship with others—any others. We are created for community. No matter how self-sufficient we think we are, we need people. When we don't get enough meaningful interaction, we're lonely.

How does God help us in our lonely times? In two big ways. First, *he* interacts with us personally. He becomes a friend to us, providing encouragement, challenge, a listening ear, and a kind of conversation. Throughout the centuries, Christians who have lived alone, either by circumstances or by choice, have reported a deepening of their spiritual lives. God has become extremely real to them, as solid a friend as any human could be. You don't have to become a monastic recluse to experience this. Just turn to God in your lonely times. Start that conversation, and see what happens.

The second thing that God does to help our loneliness is that he brings people into our lives. Sometimes lonely people connect with a church, and they're delighted with the new friendships they find. Sometimes the Lord sends certain people to cross our paths, and their love and support is exactly what we need.

Jack was feeling overworked and underappreciated one lonely night as he finished up some Internet research for his job. He got an "instant message" from Jen, a young woman he had taught years earlier. They chatted briefly online, and then she said she was headed out to a coffee shop. Would he like to join her? Yes, absolutely. They had a great talk over decaf, and they forged a fine friendship that has continued to this day. "You saved my life," Jack told Jen, only half-joking. Her timely message was a gift from God on one bleak night, and her continuing friendship keeps giving.

In lonely times, the support God provides doesn't always come from the likeliest sources. Often we find ourselves connecting with folks we'd never choose as friends ourselves, but we're needy, and God meets those needs in his own unique way.

Dear heavenly Father, I've learned that it's true that a person can feel lonely even in a crowd. Even among family members and friends, there are times I have felt terribly alone. But I'm also learning that I can find comfort and fellowship in your presence and in communion with you through prayer and by studying the Scriptures. Thank you, too, for the fellowship of others who trust in you. Help me seek them out and take the initiative to spend time with them. Perhaps some of these people struggle with feeling lonely too, and together we can chase away those feelings by enjoying our common faith in you. I ask that you would show me how to walk out of my loneliness and into all the avenues for fellowship and friendship you're providing for me.

We declare to you what we have seen and heard so that you also may have fellowship with us; and truly our fellowship is with the Father and with his Son Jesus Christ.... [I]f we walk in the light as he himself is in the light we have fellowship with one another, and the blood of Jesus his Son cleanses us from all sin.

—1 JOHN 1:3, 7

Depression

Depression has a wide range of meanings, from a brief bout of sadness to a long-term psycho-physical state. Obviously God's power can help you whenever depression has you down. In serious cases, he might use medical expertise and medication to heal you. In casual cases, he might send a new friend to cheer you up.

People can do damage when they don't understand depression. Well-meaning friends might counsel you to "turn that frown upside down," assuming that a perky attitude and a few jokes will cure you. Religious folks often see it as a spiritual problem, suggesting that the depressed person must lack a strong faith, or perhaps some hidden sin is squelching the "joy of the Lord." This can be an especially harmful approach, making you feel guilty for being depressed, which often deepens the depression.

Depression has various causes and various treatments. Sometimes it's a chemical imbalance, and sometimes that imbalance is sparked by a physiological problem. And sometimes it's part of a normal response cycle to a traumatic event. You can expect that 6 to 12 months after the death of a loved one, a person will experience depression. The second year after a divorce is similar. In the normal emotional makeup of a human being, a person recovering from emotional trauma *needs* to spend multiple months in depression. If you short-change that process, it'll just come back later. It's a bit like numbness after a physical injury; we need to shut down our feelings for a while to allow the healing to occur.

Sometimes depression results from lengthy periods of loneliness or boredom. Sometimes its roots are spiritual, as we wrestle with doubts or sins or as we seek our ultimate purpose in life.

In general, depression is marked by a deadening of emotion and a dearth of energy. Sleep and appetite suffer. Sometimes there are self-destructive impulses. Depression often feeds on itself. You don't feel like seeing people, so you cut yourself off from friends who would buoy your spirits, making you more lonely and more depressed. You don't feel like going to work, so you stay home, making you more bored and more likely to get fired, which makes you more depressed.

How does God help us in such situations? Sometimes he provides the strength to break the downward cycle. He gives us the oomph to go out with friends and have a good time, even though we lack the energy to do so on our own. Sometimes he protects us from those self-destructive impulses. Sometimes he soothes the emotional or spiritual turmoil that bothers us. Sometimes he brings people into our lives who will do any of those things for us. Often he reminds us that we are loved, that we are treasured, and that we have a purpose.

Perhaps the most famous biblical example of depression is Elijah. One day he was on a mountaintop, where he defeated an army of false prophets in a burnt-sacrifice competition. The next day the queen threatened his life, and he escaped to the desert.

There he crashed, moping, "It is enough; now, O Lord, take away my life" before falling fast asleep (1 Kings 19:4).

After Elijah awoke and journeyed farther into the desert, the Lord taught him a valuable object lesson. He sent a mighty wind, an earthquake, and a fire to pass by the cave where Elijah was, "but the Lord was not in" any of those natural displays. Then there was "a sound of sheer silence," and the Lord spoke to Elijah (verses 11–12).

Here we find a remarkable truth: *God speaks to us in the sheer silence.* Some translations have *gentle whisper,* or *still, small voice,* but the point is that we can strip away everything else—the earth, wind, and fire, even the mountaintop experience—and we can stand lonely and depressed and even suicidal in a desert cave where there is utter quiet. *And God meets us there.*

What God told Elijah in that stillness is also instructive. First, he gave him assignments—to anoint two new kings and a new prophet. Elijah's work was not finished. God's activity would continue into the next generation, and Elijah would help set that in motion. Oh, and he also informed Elijah that there were still 7,000 people in Israel who had not succumbed to idol-worship. He wasn't alone after all.

God helps us in these same ways, by letting us know we're needed to do his work in the world and by reminding us we're not alone.

Whether I'm a bit blue, in a prolonged funk, temporarily bummed, or seriously depressed, Lord God, you never leave me. You know what I need in each instance. You know how to lead me to the help and healing I need. Help me to not be afraid of reaching out to the right people for prayer and encouragement. The temptation for me is to close myself off from others, but you call me to remain in fellowship. Grant me strength and conviction to fight my impulses and to act in healing ways, rather than in hiding. But also help me be patient with the process of healing my heart, which often takes time. You know all things, Lord. Please do with me as you see fit.

Why are you downcast, O my soul?
Why so disturbed within me?
Put your hope in God,
for I will yet praise him,
my Savior and my God.
My soul is downcast within me;
therefore I will remember you.

—PSALM 42:5–6 (NIV)

Heartbreak

Few of us are immune from the pain of heartbreak. Whether it's an adolescent romance or a bitter divorce, whether a best friend moves away or a long-time partner passes away, we feel the anguish of losing a loving relationship. Pop songs and blog entries have vividly described the sensation in a thousand ways, but perhaps the most succinct is in the word itself: *heartbreak*. It feels as if the core of our being is shattered beyond repair.

When a relationship brings purpose and meaning to our lives, and that relationship is suddenly gone, we feel wounded and lost. When we discover our own value in another person's eyes, and then we lose that person, we can't help but wonder who we are. When we find delight in the company of someone else, and that company is taken away from us, we are left with deep sadness.

"I feel like she robbed me of my joy," said Kenneth, even years after his wife abandoned him. He had struggled back to a kind of normalcy, surviving the lowest lows of his emotions, but he still lacked the highs. He was okay now, but he just not very happy. His heart had been broken, and all its joy extracted from his life.

How does God help us in these situations? We receive some clues from the prophet Isaiah, who was foretelling the ministry of the Messiah:

The spirit of the Lord God is upon me,
because the Lord has anointed me;
he has sent me to bring good news to the oppressed,
to bind up the brokenhearted,
to proclaim liberty to the captives,
and release to the prisoners;

**to proclaim the year of the Lord's favor,
and the day of vengeance of our God;
to comfort all who mourn.**

—ISAIAH 61:1–2

Jesus used the above Bible verses as sort of a mission statement, and we can see many spiritual truths in Isaiah's words. For now, let's see how it applies to broken hearts:

- *"he has sent me to bring good news to the oppressed"* It may seem that your world has fallen apart, but there is still good news. You still live in a world that God has created, and we are still headed for a glorious eternity in his heavenly kingdom. The Holy Spirit regularly reminds us of these happy facts.

- *"to bind up the brokenhearted"* Well, there's our key word, but what does it mean to "bind up"? It's what you do to a wound. You wrap it, you bandage it, and you hold it together so it can heal. This suggests that the emotional numbness of the heartbroken is actually part of God's healing process. Your ability to love will grow back, but it needs to be "bound up" for a while.

- *"to proclaim liberty to the captives, and release to the prisoners"* One of the major problems of the heartbroken is that they obsess about the love they've lost. They can't break free from past memories. They feel imprisoned by the pain. God provides help by freeing them from those obsessions. He leads their minds and emotions in new directions, so they don't have to focus on their loss.

- *"to proclaim the year of the Lord's favor and the day of vengeance of our God"* The "year of the Lord's favor" is a specific reference to an Israelite tradition—a festive year of freedom and restoration—but the phrasing might give us additional insight. One of the worst things about lost love is that we don't feel loved. This phrase reminds us that the Lord continues to favor us, and the Spirit proclaims that fact to us. We are loved by the Lord himself. But sometimes heartbreak comes with anger attached, often in the case of divorce or romantic breakups. The Spirit also proclaims that the Lord can take care of the vengeance, so we don't have to. We can let go of our hatred and get on with our healing.

- *"to comfort all who mourn."* Many believers who have experienced heartbreak will testify to the value of the Spirit's comfort. That gentle whisper comes through the sheer silence—*you are loved; you will get through this; you will heal; I still have big plans for you, so rest now; have a good cry, but remember always that I love you.*

Dear Lord, I come to you when I have no one else. When I feel abandoned by everyone who matters to me, I know I can count on you. Heal my hurting heart. Whisper your love to me in that still, small voice—and give me the ears to hear it. Break through my self-pity to remind me that you still care for me. Bring your comfort into the stark realities of my life. Bind up my broken heart so I can return to wholeness. Salve my wounds so I can serve you once again. Amen.

Chapter 8
HEALTH PLAN

It seems as though the most important issue in the news media is health. Politically, it's the question of health insurance. Financially, it's the rising cost of health care. Socially, we're constantly encouraged to eat a healthier diet and exercise more. Medically, we get frantic updates on the H1N1 flu and other pandemics. And we keep seeing those TV commercials for drugs that treat all sorts of embarrassing ailments (and they hope we won't notice the long list of negative side effects). Health is all the rage.

Our society *is* aging. That's what happens when medical care improves and people live longer. In many ways, this is a good problem to have, but suddenly millions more people have health concerns that go along with aging.

Of course, it's not just the elderly who get sick. Illness touches us all at one point or another, whether we're old or young. At such times, we pray for the sick. We ask God to apply his healing power, and sometimes that clearly happens with miraculous recoveries. But often the recovery is rather ordinary, part of the normal cycle of life. And sometimes sick people get worse and die, even when they're prayed for. So how do we make sense of all this? How should we pray for the sick, and how does God help?

I ask you neither for health nor for sickness, for life nor for death; but that you may dispose of my health and my sickness, my life and my death, for your glory.... You alone know what is expedient for me; you are the sovereign master, do with me according to your will. Give to me, or take away from me, only conform my will to yours. I know but one thing, Lord, that it is good to follow you, and bad to offend you. Apart from that, I know not what is good or bad in anything. I know not which is most profitable to me, health or sickness, wealth or poverty, nor anything else in the world. That discernment is beyond the power of men or angels, and is hidden among the secrets of your providence, which I adore, but do not seek to fathom.

—BLAISE PASCAL

Dear Father in heaven, the mysteries of your purposes escape my understanding. They puzzle and perplex me. That's why I need faith in who you are to shore up what I don't always understand about what you do: why you choose to heal in some instances and not in others; why a miracle comes to one person in answer to prayer, while another person's illness persists even though earnest petitions for healing are offered up to you. These questions baffle me. And yet, because I know you are wise and good and that your love is unfailing, I can put myself in your hands, come what may. But I will always ask for healing, since you invite me to cast my cares on you, for I believe with all my heart that you do care for me.

For everything there is a season, and a time for every matter under heaven: a time to be born, and a time to die;...a time to kill, and a time to heal;...a time to weep, and a time to laugh; a time to mourn, and a time to dance.

—ECCLESIASTES 3:1–4

Saving the Sick

The Book of James offers an interesting perspective: "The prayer of faith will save the sick, and the Lord will raise them up; and anyone who has committed sins will be forgiven. Therefore confess your sins to one another, and pray for one another, so that you may be healed. The prayer of the righteous is powerful and effective" (James 5:15–16).

The word for *save* in the first line of this passage has multiple meanings—both spiritual salvation and physical healing. Restoration to health is associated with the forgiveness of sin. Prayer is "powerful and effective" both because it brings about healing and because it draws people closer to God.

Granted, some people take the connection too far. Some churches assume that all sickness is a result of the sick person's sin. You're afraid to sniffle, for fear that they'll suspect some moral failing in your life. Similarly, some Christians refuse to see doctors, assuming that every illness is basically spiritual. Sin is the problem and faith is the solution, as they see it, and medical science misses the point.

We don't need to make this an "either/or" issue. Sickness is a physical condition that often has spiritual components. We can and should pray for physical healing. We want people to come back to health, to resume their place in our lives, and to enjoy life to its fullest. But the words from James remind us that there's a spiritual side to the matter as well. We should also be praying for the souls of those people who are ailing. God is interested in healing both body *and* spirit.

Donna's life was falling apart before she ever got "the diagnosis." Her marriage was in trouble, her career suffering, and her finances a mess. That's when her pastor challenged her to give those troubles over to God. *Surrender* was the term he used, and she began to apply it. She learned that she could trust God to manage her life better than she could.

Did her problems instantly go away? Not exactly. Soon after that, she was diagnosed with cancer. Ironically, though, her *spiritual* healing had already begun. Her health issues were just new things to turn over to God. She knew she could trust him to be there for her through all the chemo and radiation treatments.

It was a long haul. There were advances and then setbacks. Over the following years, she had several rounds of the debilitating treatments, but she had a church full of faithful friends praying for her. During times of remission, she would regain her strength enough to join them in worship. At one point, she even headed up the church's care ministry, providing food, transportation, and visits to others who were sick. Nurses began to notice that, while all the other cancer patients were anxious or even bitter, and understandably so, Donna was vibrant and joyous. She wasn't denying the existence of the disease, but she had given it to her Lord. Why should it keep her from living a dynamic life that would glorify him?

And that's where she is now, in remission, trusting God, helping others. The prayers of her many friends are being answered—not just in the forestalling of the disease but also in the exalting of her spirit. She has been able to live life more fully than most healthy people, and God has given her the power to do that.

Thank you, Lord God, for the gifts of health and life. I never cherish these more than when I'm confronted with the possibilities and realities of serious illness or death. But even when I'm well, help me remember to be grateful for the precious gift of wellness. And when I'm ill, remind me that I can call out to you for healing and for strength to endure until healing comes, whether that healing is in this life or in the one that's to come. Thank you for your power at work in my life, giving me exactly what I need, just when I need it.

The wish for healing has ever been the half of health.

—SENECA, *HIPPOLYTUS*

Bless the Lord, O my soul, and all that is within me, bless his holy name. Bless the Lord, O my soul, and do not forget all his benefits—who forgives all your iniquity, who heals all your diseases, who redeems your life from the Pit, who crowns you with steadfast love and mercy, who satisfies you with good as long as you live so that your youth is renewed like the eagle's.

—PSALM 103:1–5

Now and Then

You might say we all suffer from a terminal condition. It's called humanity. We may have decades to live or just months—we don't know. No one knows. Whether we're disease-ridden or perfectly healthy, we could die tomorrow. Or we could live for years and years. In any case, our bodies are in the process of decay. We are dying even as we're living.

But one thing we do know: Physical death is not the end. We believe in eternal life—an existence that awaits us in God's presence, after we have shuffled off this mortal coil. To be absent from the body is to be present with the Lord. We look forward to a forever without sickness or sorrow. Not that we're in a big hurry to get there. We still cling to our earthly lives tenaciously, but we need not be overly daunted by death.

The Apostle Paul displayed a similar ambivalence in his letter to the Philippians. Writing from prison, he thought he might die soon. "It is my eager expectation and hope that . . . Christ will be exalted now as always in my body, whether by life or by death. For to me, living is Christ and dying is gain. If I am to live in the flesh, that means fruitful labor for me; and I do not know which I prefer. I am hard pressed between the two: my desire is to depart and be with Christ, for that is far better; but to remain in the flesh is more necessary for you" (Philippians 1:20–24).

Physical death held no threat for him. He only worried that he'd no longer be able to help his friends if he had moved on to his eternal reward and they hadn't. As a result, he was torn between desire and necessity, between now and then. This dilemma that

Paul expressed can actually help us as we pray for those who are seriously ill, or as we seek help from God for our own illnesses. There is nothing wrong with wanting to live, or wanting our loved ones to keep living. This is not a lack of faith, but a perfectly acceptable emotion, and we should have no hesitation in praying for physical healing.

The restoration of earthly life is a blessing to loved ones, and it may allow more "fruitful labor," in Paul's terms. But at the same time, physical death is not a tragedy for the believer. While loved ones grieve the fact that they are parted from the deceased, they should understand that it is "far better" for the person to "depart and be with Christ." It's a win-win.

See, the home of God is among mortals. He will dwell with them; they will be his peoples, and God himself will be with them; he will wipe every tear from their eyes. Death will be no more; mourning and crying and pain will be no more, for the first things have passed away.

—REVELATION 21:3–4

Thank you, Lord, for the freedom to talk to you honestly about any situation in my life. It helps that your Word shows me the Apostle Paul's dilemma about life and death. It is kind of like Hamlet's question: "To be, or not to be?" Only, in Paul's case, he asks a similar question, not out of depression, but because he was torn between two blessed realities: one of fruitful ministry and the other of being with you in paradise. I struggle with life and death, too! At times, I don't want to let go of loved ones because I care so much for them, and yet I know that to them, in their intense suffering, it would be a great blessing for them to go and finally be with you. Life and death is in your hands, dear Lord. That is where I put myself as well. Your will be done.

Kingdom Come

Jesus taught us to pray, "Your kingdom come. Your will be done, on earth as it is in heaven" (Matthew 6:10). Because of this, many Christians have learned to attach "if it be your will" to their prayers, recognizing that God might want something quite different from what they're praying for. This tagline can serve as a helpful reminder to us that we ultimately need to surrender to God's desires, but Scripture gives us every indication that God enjoys hearing about *our* desires. He wants to hear our requests.

Meanwhile, that other phrase from the Lord's Prayer, "thy kingdom come," is fascinating. When we say that, what are we actually praying for? Are we asking God to hasten the Second Coming? Maybe. But we might also be asking God to bring the benefits of his future kingdom into the present. And one of those benefits is that God's kingdom will be free of sickness. So when we pray for physical healing, we know that God will grant that request in his coming kingdom, but we're asking for it in advance. We're asking for this benefit of the kingdom to come a bit sooner so that the healing might not occur then, but now.

Sometimes, in answer to our prayers, God chooses to do this. Sometimes he doesn't. Sometimes he brings future healing into the present, allowing a person to enjoy earthly life a little longer. Sometimes he prefers to bring someone into his presence right away.

I do want your will for all things in my life, heavenly Father, especially when it comes to my deepest desires to see healing in my life and in the lives of those I care most about. Honestly, when you choose not to heal and you take someone from me, it hurts beyond words. You know that I've even been angry with you when things haven't gone the way I'd hoped. But after I've regained perspective, Father, I really do trust that your plan is best and that you know when to take someone home to be with you and when not to. Your kingdom come, Lord! Heal where healing is needed, carry home those whose time has come to be with you, sustain those who must endure illness, and ultimately heal us all—to the praise of your grace and love.

Heal me, O Lord, and I shall be healed; save me, and I shall be saved; for you are my praise.

—JEREMIAH 17:14

How Does God Help?

We've seen how "healing" is a much bigger issue than we usually think. It happens fully in God's future kingdom, but it sometimes occurs in the present. It also involves both body and spirit. There are times when God allows a person to succumb to sickness, but provides faith, forgiveness, and blessing on the deathbed. We might look for one kind of miracle and get another.

God helps us by providing strength and endurance in times of physical pain. He provides peace amid the insecurity of a serious illness. He gives us the courage to say things that must be said to friends and loved ones. He often gives inexplicable joy in the face of extreme circumstances. And he opens our eyes to see what's most important.

Let's not forget the ways God uses other people to help us. He certainly uses the skills of doctors and hospital staff to achieve his healing, but he especially works through the community of faith, as people rally around a sick person. Often relationships are forged or strengthened as one person helps another who is ill. This is love in action.

We should pray for a sane mind in a sound body.

—JUVENAL, *SATIRES*

O Lord my God, I cried to you for help, and you have healed me.... To you, O Lord, I cried, and to the Lord I made supplication: "What profit is there in my death, if I go down to the Pit? Will the dust praise you? Will it tell of your faithfulness? Hear, O Lord, and be gracious to me! O Lord be my helper!"

—PSALM 30:2, 8–10

Chapter 9

"Unless the Lord Builds the House…"

Main Street USA. The name captured a concept for this combination of homes and shops in Middle America. It was the late 1980s, and folks were growing weary of the dog-eat-dog world. They longed for good old-fashioned *community,* and this new development would give it to them. Upscale condos and apartments would face restaurants and stores across a lovely pedestrian boulevard. People would never have to leave. This place would have everything they needed.

Except a church.

One day as Jeff drove past this emerging development, that thought struck him. *Where's the church?* He believes God put that question into his head. *They thought of every other human need—why didn't they think of their spiritual needs?* That was the beginning of a big idea that grew over the following months . . . and decades. *We need to start a church.*

It was an exciting thought for Jeff, as well as a terrifying one. He was just an associate pastor at a church a few towns away. He didn't know anything about starting a church, but he did know he needed God's help, and lots of it. If God was leading him in this direction, God would have to show the way. Jeff and his wife began praying about this idea. Jeff shared it with the senior minister at his church, who joined them in prayer. Friends and family were enlisted as prayer partners as well. This was an audacious venture, and only God could make it happen.

Immediately there were problems. They wouldn't be able to meet in the Main Street complex. There was some talk about starting in a different area, but soon they focused on a newly built elementary school a few miles from Main Street. Its all-purpose room would be an ideal meeting place, and school officials were cooperative.

Now meeting regularly for prayer and planning with a dozen core members of this new church enterprise, Jeff set his sights on a launch date of April 1. The group mobilized a publicity push, including a massive phone campaign, targeting that date.

April fools!

Days before the phone calls were made, the school announced that its facility would not be available until the fall. It was a momentum-killer. Plans had to be scrapped and reassembled, and the core group had to mark time until November. *Why, God, why?* That was the tone of prayers launched by the core group in the following months. *We thought you were guiding us to do this, Lord. Are you?*

Soon, however, they realized that the delay was a blessing. The intervening months allowed better planning, greater cohesion in the group, and more prayer. Above all, it was a reminder that they were not in control—not Jeff, not the core group. God was.

In November, the church was launched with 289 in attendance. It has grown steadily ever since. Committed to welcoming "seekers" into a vibrant relationship with God, this church has helped hundreds along that journey of faith. Challenges have arisen along the way, but the congregation has consistently looked to the Lord for help and have received it.

Oh, and nine years after their launch, they built their own building, a stone's throw from the Main Street complex where the idea was hatched.

"Unless the Lord builds the house, those who build it labor in vain" (Psalm 127:1). Members of that church will confirm the truth of that verse. Besides the startup of the church itself, they have begun numerous church-sponsored enterprises along the way—food distribution, arts programs, a coffee shop, and a craft show—and the lesson they consistently learn is this: *We are not in control; God is.* And they will also tell you that whenever they stop looking for God's help, their plans crash and burn.

This could be an important lesson for you in whatever enterprises you're involved with. So far we've been discussing God's help in various crisis situations, but what about positive situations when you're stepping out in some new venture? Are you launching a business, beginning a new ministry at your church, starting a family, perhaps even guiding your child into a new activity? What kind of help will God give you in those situations, and how can you access it?

"God helps those who help themselves." You've heard that saying, but is it really true? Is it the best way to look at things? It seems to be the sort of thing you'd say to some couch potato who complains, "I asked God to get me a job, and he hasn't, so I just stay home and watch *Springer*." In that case, it makes sense. *Get up. Get busy. Don't sit around waiting for a divine lightning bolt when you already know what you need to do!*

But there are other people who use this adage to move ahead with their own plans, paying little heed to what God wants. They "help themselves," doing whatever they think best, and they assume that God will bless them. Somewhere between those two extremes is our best position. We should say, "God helps those who rely on his help and are willing to use his help courageously." The truth of the matter is that God is ready to help us at every stage of a new enterprise, and we would do well to ask for his aid.

God Helps Us Clarify the Vision

Any new project starts with a vision of what needs to happen and what can be achieved. God often puts these visions into our heads, as he did with Jeff in identifying the absence of a church in that "ideal" community. For you, it might be a completely different vision:

"What can we do to help the unemployed in our community?"

"If I go back to school and get a degree, will I work more effectively?"

"Perhaps I could buy that building on the corner and start a business."

"Do I have a good enough voice to join the community chorus?"

Perhaps thoughts like these go through your head all the time. If so, converse with God, and when you do, you'll recognize the times when he's nudging you forward. Is there a need you're suddenly noticing? Is there a talent you're suddenly discovering in yourself? Does the Lord seem to be bringing together the right people and resources for a new venture? Don't ignore these thoughts. Don't dismiss them as fanciful musing. If the idea is coming from God, he'll confirm it and refine it.

Dear heavenly Father, when I'm eager to get going on some vision I believe you have given me, help me to not run ahead of you. And when it seems as if I'm being thwarted, help me remember that "thwarting" can be a part of your timing. I ask that you would grant me peace in the process, trust in your timing, willingness to wait, and sensitivity to your Spirit's leading. I want to be a good follower, especially when I find myself in a position of leadership. May I always look to you at all times for everything. Amen.

God Helps Us Redeem Bad Situations

Ironically, comprehending God's vision for our lives is often clearest when we've had our hopes dashed.

Many people have started successful businesses after being laid off or fired. "I always dreamed of working for myself, but I never would have had the guts," says one such entrepreneur. "But I was suddenly out of a job and needed to do *something*." Desperation is the mother of creativity. When the doors of your life are closing, look around to see what God has opened. God might be turning evil into good.

The Old Testament character of Joseph is the poster child for this kind of transformation. Sold as a slave by jealous brothers, he became head servant. Falsely accused and imprisoned, he became the prison trustee. Throughout a string of misfortunes, he kept finding new ways to practice his God-given abilities until, amazingly, he was interpreting dreams for the most powerful man in Egypt.

Joseph said to [his brothers], "Do not be afraid! Am I in the place of God? Even though you intended to do harm to me, God intended it for good, in order to preserve a numerous people, as he is doing today."

—GENESIS 50:19–20

God Helps Us Make Effective Plans

"The plans of the diligent lead surely to abundance, but everyone who is hasty comes only to want" (Proverbs 21:5). Don't think you can wing it, just because God gave you an idea. Even Jesus talked about the importance of counting the cost before embarking on a building project (see Luke 14:28). God will guide you, but you need to be diligent in making plans.

At this stage, God's help takes many forms. He inspires creative solutions to some problems that might squelch the project from the start. He sharpens our minds to anticipate obstacles before they occur. He calms us down enough to get a realistic look at the situation, so our projections are neither optimistic nor pessimistic. He strengthens us against the naysayers. It's important to stay in touch with God through the planning process.

My plans may seem great to me and to others, Lord God, but unless they are in line with your purposes, ultimately they won't succeed. As I look to you for direction, guidance, inspiration, and wisdom, I pray that you would grant me ears to hear and eyes to see what you are revealing to me. I pray that I would be obedient, too, and follow as you show me the steps to take.

God Helps Us Choose Valuable Teammates

Any important enterprise you begin will require help from others. They might be business consultants, accountants, or Web designers. They might be church folks with the gifts of serving, teaching, or administration. If your new enterprise is starting a family, your team is not just you and your spouse, but parents, in-laws, and potential babysitters. You can't go it alone in any of these pursuits.

"I'm thinking of going back to school for a master's degree," said one man who was about to turn 50. It was a crazy idea in many ways, but his sister was within earshot, and she took him seriously. "Do you really mean that?" she asked. "Because if you do, I'll help you. I'll check up on you to see if you're choosing a good program, to see if you're completing the application, and so on. I don't want to nag you, but if you need my encouragement along the way, I'll be there for you."

The truth was, he'd been musing about grad school for years, but he never had a teammate before. Now, with his sister's encouragement, he found a school, applied, and eventually earned his degree.

Here's one hint about choosing teammates. God loves to surprise us. He doesn't always select the people we'd select, but he's constantly matching people to the tasks that will help them grow. Tune in to God's values as you build your team, and you'll be delighted by the result.

Dear Lord, it is in the context of teamwork that we learn to appreciate the way you have gifted your people, each one individually equipped to carry out a special aspect of your mission. I pray you will bring them my way or send me their way. Please build this team as only you know how to do, and help me do what you have called me to do in a way that will truly glorify your Son, Jesus Christ.

Two are better than one, because they have a good reward for their toil. For if they fall, one will lift up the other; but woe to one who is alone and falls and does not have another to help...and though one might prevail against another, two will withstand one. A threefold cord is not quickly broken.

—ECCLESIASTES 4:9–10, 12

God Helps Us Work Hard

It seemed like such a good idea when Gail tried out for the community theater. She was becoming aware of new talents and decided to try them out. It was even more exciting when she landed a substantial role. What she hadn't expected was the demanding schedule—not only learning all those lines, songs, and dances but also practicing three nights a week, until the final week, when the director flatly said, "We own you." Then, already worn out, they had long rehearsals every night until they finally opened the play, hoping that sheer adrenaline would fuel their performance. It was the hardest Gail had ever worked in her life, but God had given her the strength.

If you start your own business, be ready for 18-hour days. If you go back to school, you'll be cramming study time and class time into the schedule you already keep. If you launch a ministry at church, you can expect too much work with too few volunteers. If you're starting a family—well, you really weren't expecting to get any sleep in the next year, were you?

Whatever your new enterprise is, it will involve hard work. Your body, mind, and emotions will be stretched to their limit. But if God has led you into this, he will see you through it. "He gives power to the faint, and strengthens the powerless," the prophet Isaiah promised. "Those who wait for the Lord shall renew their strength, they shall mount up with wings like eagles, they shall run and not be weary, they shall walk and not faint" (Isaiah 40:29, 31).

I look to you, my Lord, for the strength and ability to do the work that is before me—to do it well, to do it with integrity, and to do it to your honor and glory. May it always be acceptable in your sight. I commit my time and energies to you now. Please bless them and multiply them as you did the loaves and fishes that day by the seashore. I pray for efficiency and diligence so this work will go well in blessing many lives. Thank you, Lord. Amen.

I have always thought that one man of tolerable abilities may work great changes, and accomplish great affairs among mankind, if he first forms a good plan, and, cutting off all amusements or other employments that would divert his attention, make the execution of that same plan his sole study and business.

—BENJAMIN FRANKLIN

God Helps Us Deal with Failure

New enterprises involve risk, and there's always a risk of failure. Sometimes we assume that, if God leads us into a project, he guarantees success. Not exactly. God works through successes and failures alike. Sometimes he leads us in a straight line, but usually it's a zigzag route. In fact, we tend to learn more when things don't work out well, and sometimes we can see the next step of our faith journey only because we stumbled on the last one.

Consider the plans of the Apostle Paul on his second missionary trip. He was convinced that God wanted him to revisit the places where he had planted churches on his first trip, along with his associate Barnabas. But he and Barnabas had a falling-out, so Paul had to scramble to find a new partner, Silas. There was trouble even before the trip starts.

Subsequently, Paul and Silas returned to the old places, and then what? Let's pick up the travelogue from Acts 16 (but in case your eyes glaze over when you read unpronounceable place-names, we'll paraphrase some of those). "They went through [one region] and [another], having been forbidden by the Holy Spirit to speak the word in Asia. . . . They attempted to go into [another inland region], but the Spirit of Jesus did not allow them, so . . . they went down to [the seaport]. During the night Paul had a vision: there stood a man of Macedonia pleading with him and saying, 'Come over to Macedonia and help us.'" (see Acts 16:6–9).

Go through those verses again step by step, and imagine Paul's frustration. *Can't go here; can't go there. What do you want from me, Lord? Did I totally mess up in that argument with Barnabas? Is there anywhere I can preach the gospel?* It's quite possible that he went to the seaport to catch a boat going home. Was he calling off the mission? That's when God sent a new vision to Paul, from an area he hadn't even thought of yet—Macedonia, which is in Europe. He was still working in Asia Minor, but when all those other possibilities failed, only then was he ready for a new vision.

So if you've launched into some courageous enterprise and it hasn't gone well, don't give up. See if your failure has brought you to a place where you can receive a new vision. Let God pick you up and send you somewhere new.

This one thing I do: forgetting what lies behind and straining forward to what lies ahead, I press on toward the goal for the prize of the heavenly call of God in Christ Jesus.

—PHILIPPIANS 3:13–14

Failure has taken the wind out of my sails, Lord. I hadn't thought of looking for a new vision. Failing has a way of making me feel as though I shouldn't try again. But if this is merely a redirection from you, a pointing to something else, then help me, Lord, to perceive it. Open my eyes to be able to see it, and please grant me the courage and conviction to begin again. In your holy name, I pray. Amen.

Failure after long perseverance is much grander than never to have a striving good enough to be called a failure.

—GEORGE ELIOT

God Helps Us Deal with Success

Peter walked on water. We forget that sometimes. This apostle was always blurting out wrong answers in his desire to be the best and to be Jesus' favorite. And one night, on a stormy sea, he succeeded. He saw Jesus walking on the waves, and he stepped out to meet him. The other disciples were cowering in the boat, but Peter set himself apart once and for all. He was the only disciple who dared to defy nature and stand with Jesus. Only *he* had the necessary faith— until he didn't.

When he lost his focus on Jesus, Peter began to sink.

Success carries dangers we seldom anticipate. God may lead us into some activity, and we may do well until we lose focus. For example, some TV preachers primarily focus on money and worldly pleasures after gaining tremendous popularity. Some ministry leaders spend so much time doing God's work that their families are neglected. Some pastors push their churches to be bigger, better, trendier, and leave parishioners wounded and broken along the way. Some business leaders, who started out in prayer, now cheat, lie, and steal in order to gain a greater market share. Some artists, who came to fame with soul-stirring masterpieces, now produce shallow fare to keep the public happy. Some parents, who dedicated their children to the Lord, now pressure them to win at any cost in pageants and sports.

When we lose our focus on Jesus, we invariably sink.

If we stay in touch with the Lord, he can help us avoid the soul-destructive dangers of success. He keeps us humble and loving. He reminds us of what's most important.

For the believer, any new venture needs to be saturated with prayer. Get your friends and relatives praying. Set aside special times in your own schedule to communicate with God. You're not just asking for some kind of rubber-stamp "blessing" on your work. You need his ongoing help, as you envision the enterprise and plan it, as you build your team and deploy them, and as you work harder than you've ever worked before. You need him to keep guiding you both when you fail and when you succeed.

"Let the one who boasts boast in the Lord." For it is not those who commend themselves that are approved, but those whom the Lord commends.

—2 CORINTHIANS 10:17–18

Dear Lord, I dedicate this new enterprise to you. More than that, I offer it to you. I invite you to join me in this effort. Imagine it with me. Let's put your creativity and mine together to figure out the best way to make this happen. I rely on your guidance as I step forward on this path. Show me the people you want me to work with. Use me in their lives and use them in mine to encourage, challenge, and build up each other. Help me bounce back from failure and to stay grounded in success. I devote all of this to your glory. Amen.

Chapter 10
Asking for It

A father was in the car with his 5-year-old son when fog rolled in. Driving became worrisome, to say the least. The father thought about pulling over, but he wasn't sure where "over" was. It seemed best to keep moving slowly forward, following the white lines and scanning the few feet he could see in front of him.

The boy saw his father tense up, and he became worried too. "Are we gonna be okay?" he asked.

"You know what's good to do in situations like this?" the dad replied. "We can pray. We can ask God to help us out of this mess, and we can trust him to make it okay."

And there on a foggy road, a father taught his son to pray. With his eyes never leaving the highway, the man voiced the prayer for both of them—that God would keep them safe, that he would roll away the fog, and that he would keep the father alert while he drove. The boy said, "Amen."

A few minutes later the fog began to dissipate. They made it home safely.

Fast-forward a few years. That same boy has a younger brother who takes a tumble and gets knocked out. Frantic, the mother lays her unconscious son in the back seat and drives to the hospital. The older son, sitting beside her, sees her anxiety and says calmly, "It'll be okay, mom. You do the driving, and I'll do the praying."

It's a lesson we all can learn. God wants us to ask him for help, not only in crises but in our daily challenges as well. We can trust him to make things "okay"—not that every situation will go the way we want, but that God will be involved in our concern. He will provide strength, peace, and insight.

Oh, by the way, the unconscious boy awoke on the examining table, looked up, and said, "Hiya, Doc." He was fine. In fact, he grew up to write this book.

We have reviewed the many ways that God helps us in the various situations in which we need help, and though each situation is different, there's one common thread: It's important for us to *ask for his help.* It's hard to overstate the importance of this simple act. Asking is an act of faith. By doing this, we acknowledge that we lack the resources to help ourselves and that God has the power to assist us. Such faith also trusts in God's love for us.

Some people say, "I feel weird about asking God for favors for myself. It seems selfish." That might be understandable if you're asking for a new car, but if you need a new job because your last one was downsized, that isn't a selfish prayer at all.

Others seem determined to help themselves before asking God to help them, but this is exactly the kind of attitude that got the Pharisees in trouble. They felt secure in their own spiritual resources and refused to ask God for help. This pride kept them from tapping into God's grace.

God wants us to ask for his help. He longs for us to reach out to him. "Call to me and I will answer you," God says to us (Jeremiah 33:3). The prophet Isaiah portrays God holding out his hands, crying out, "Here I am, here I am" to people who had ignored him (Isaiah 65:1). God cries out to us as well when we have forgotten him.

More things are wrought by prayer
Than this world dreams of.

—LORD TENNYSON, "THE PASSING OF ARTHUR,"
IDYLLS OF THE KING

Dear Lord, you've heard me say these words before—"All I can do now is pray"—when someone has been in dire straits and I have exhausted all other ways to help. And yet, it's now clear to me that my viewpoint is faulty when I think and speak that way. Prayer *is* the best thing—not just some last resort for help—that I can be doing for anyone at any time. Forgive me for minimizing or diminishing the significance of this blessed means of approaching you—the Almighty God. I want to pray more. I want to grow in my understanding of what it means to pray well. I know it doesn't have to do with fancy speech or a perfect track record. Rather, Lord, you receive those who come to you with honest and humble hearts. Thank you for your boundless mercy.

Ask, and it will be given you; search, and you will find; knock, and the door will be opened for you. For everyone who asks receives, and everyone who searches finds, and for everyone who knocks, the door will be opened. Is there anyone among you who, if your child asks for bread, will give a stone? Or if the child asks for a fish, will give a snake? If you then, who are evil, know how to give good gifts to your children, how much more will your Father in heaven give good things to those who ask him!

—MATTHEW 7:7–11

How to Ask God for Help

Ask humbly. God is God, and you aren't. He doesn't owe you anything. In fact, he thundered to Job the rhetorical question: "Who has a claim against me that

I must pay? Everything under heaven belongs to me"
(Job 41:11 NIV). Give him the respect that's due him.

Ask boldly. While this might seem to contradict the
previous point, we're invited to "approach the throne
of grace with boldness" (Hebrews 4:16). While we
humbly recognize our position as servants of the
Most High God, we are also welcomed as his children
and heirs. Thus we need not be timid when communi-
cating our needs.

Ask openly. Be honest about your feelings and
desires. There's no use playing games with God. He'll
see through any attempt at manipulation. Lay your
heart bare before the gaze of the Almighty, and see
how he responds.

Ask, and listen. Prayer is a conversation, and we can
learn a lot as we listen to God's responses. We can tell
him what we want, and he can tell us what we need.
We can share our vision of where the future needs
to go, and he can share his. If we're not completely
open with our requests, we won't be able to see how
he transforms them. This can be a life-changing
opportunity for us, if we fully engage in this process
of communication.

Be thankful. When we ask for God's help, we start with the understanding that he has helped us before. We stand where we are because of his abundant grace. It only makes sense to blanket our prayers with an attitude of gratitude. Paul tells us, "... with thanksgiving let your requests be made known to God" (Philippians 4:6).

Expect to be amazed. Remember that our God "is able to accomplish abundantly far more than all we can ask or imagine" (Ephesians 3:20). He works miracles, even today.

Give ear to my words, O Lord; give heed to my sighing. Listen to the sound of my cry, my King and my God, for to you I pray. O Lord, in the morning you hear my voice; in the morning I plead my case to you.... I, through the abundance of your steadfast love, will enter your house. I will bow down toward your holy temple in awe of you.

—PSALM 5:1–3, 7

Prayer enlarges the heart until it is capable of containing God's gift of himself.

—MOTHER TERESA

Heavenly Father, you invite me to come into your presence and to communicate with you through prayer. What an awesome privilege! As I consider this honor, I realize that I want to come to you not only with reverence and respect but also with the abandon of a child, for that is what I am! It seems like a delicate balance to strike, and I'm not sure how to do it. Please keep me from bringing my arrogance and flippancy before you. Instead, may I come to you with awe and adoration and with an awareness of your holiness and also of your Father's heart. Search my own heart, and help me come to you with a heart full of love and devotion.

How God Answers

Can we draw any generalizations about how God helps us? We've looked at specific types of needs, but are there any overarching patterns? Maybe a few. We never want to put God in a box, telling him what he can and cannot do, but it might help us to know what sort of miracles to look for.

God helps us according to his own timing. We want help *now,* because we need to get on with our lives, but God doesn't work according to our schedules and priorities. Sometimes we think he's not answering, or that he doesn't care, merely because he seems to be delaying his responses to our prayer requests. The Bible speaks often of the importance of "waiting for the Lord." When his friend Lazarus became fatally ill, Jesus did not rush to his side, but waited a few days, and Lazarus's sister became very upset. Yet Jesus did an even greater miracle, raising Lazarus from the dead. "As the heavens are higher than the earth," the Lord says, "so are my ways higher than your ways" (Isaiah 55:9). We can trust him to do the right thing at the right time.

God offers help in many natural ways. Our Creator has already established systems of healing and restoration in our world and in our bodies. We seldom crow about a "miraculous healing" from a common cold, because it's . . . well, common. The problem is minor and it goes away "on its own." Actually that's God at work, too, but we tend to overlook it because his work was eons ago when he fashioned human DNA. We should keep this in mind, especially when we seek his help for various health concerns. You can ask God to lower your blood pressure, but you can also skip that double cheeseburger for lunch. God doesn't demand that we always be passive. Seek God, but also see a doctor.

God provides help through us and other people. Surely you've heard the story of the man whose neighborhood was flooded. He sat on the roof and prayed for God's help. A fire truck came by with an offer to drive him to safety, but no, he was trusting God to save him. As the waters rose, some neighbors rowed past and invited him into their boat, but no. Then a helicopter hovered, but the man declined, declaring his trust in God. When he finally drowned and went to heaven, he asked God, "Why didn't you save me?"

The Lord replied, "I sent a truck, a boat, and a helicopter. What more do you want?"

The Lord's assistance often comes to us through other people, whether they're believers or not, whether we like them or not. Similarly, God often asks us to provide help for others. This is one way he works his miracles.

God chooses unlikely instruments. God chose a shepherd boy to be Israel's greatest king. He chose a peasant girl to bear the Messiah. He chose the church's worst enemy to be their best missionary. He is full of surprises. He chose the godless nation of Babylon to punish Israel for idolatry, a fact with which several prophets had a hard time. He chose to use persecution to force the young church out of Jerusalem. Our God is an artist with many colors on his palette. Don't dismiss any person or event; he can use them all.

God sometimes works secretly. There will be a time when God's greatness is trumpeted throughout the universe. It is then that we will participate in raucous praise, and there are even times here on earth that we will celebrate God's awesome deeds, but a lot of God's work flies under the radar. He has always worked this way, making subtle changes in people's hearts, wooing them softly, effecting intricate changes in situations that add up to major differences. Look back at the biggest things God has done for you, and you'll probably see combinations of tiny adjustments that you may have overlooked at the time.

God helps us in ways that help us grow. We need to remember that God isn't trying to give us a pain-free life. His goal is our spiritual growth. He wants to draw us ever closer to him, transforming us into the image of his Son, Jesus Christ. Sometimes this process is compared to smelting, where metal is fired up to brutal temperatures in order to purify it. In the same way, sometimes we feel as if we're in a blast furnace. We want the troubles to go away, but that might not be God's main aim. He will help us by standing with us in the furnace, by strengthening our hearts, and by giving us inexplicable joy.

I will bless the Lord at all times; his praise shall continually be in my mouth. My soul makes its boast in the Lord; let the humble hear and be glad. O magnify the Lord with me, and let us exalt his name together. I sought the Lord and he answered me, and delivered me from all my fears. Look to him, and be radiant; so your faces shall never be ashamed.

—PSALM 34:1–5

*Prayer should be the key of the day
and the lock of the night.*

—THOMAS FULLER, *GNOMOLOGIA*

Dear Lord, I want to grow in you. Use
my current difficulties to teach me, to
develop me, to toughen me, and to
soften me. Draw my heart closer to
your heart. I rely on you for help in
a hundred ways—emotional support,
financial need, relationship issues, and so
on. I beg you to walk with me through
life, transforming each situation. Let your
amazing power change the things that
trouble me, but let it also change me.
And let me bask in your amazing love. In
Jesus' wondrous name, I pray. Amen.